How to Write a Single Page Resume

It's Not Just What You Say, But How You Say It That Counts

by Ed Bagley

The Chief Writer and Marketer for Quality-Resumes-by-Ed-Bagley.com

Dedication

This book is dedicated to my mother, **Mildred Louise Baker**. She learned survival skills in the workplace without the benefit of a job-hunting resource like this. This book is also dedicated to my maternal grandparents, **Edward and Amelia Baker**. Edward Louis Baker, my namesake, was a self-taught man of integrity, decency and honesty, who lived his life as a happy man, secure in his final destiny. Amelia Baker, a simple woman of great faith and compassion, was the most other-centered person I have ever known. I was raised by my grandparents during the first 5 years of my life. Everything good I ever learned in my life I learned from my grandparents during those first 5 years, and I remain grateful to this day 62 years later (4-20-12) for their love, patience, faith, compassion and understanding. For many of us, one of our greatest gifts in life was our grandparents.

A Short Note Before We Get Started . . .

This book happened as a result of my more than 5,400 active clients pressing me for more and better information on repositioning themselves in the economy following a merger, acquisition, restructuring or downsizing. Before they found me, many of them had been to a bookstore to buy publications on resume writing, and had become more confused about the process *after* they had read the how-to book.

The fact is that many such books give a synopsis up front of do's and don'ts and then present several resume and cover letter examples for people to follow. This encourages clients to copycat what they see without any understanding of the thought process and belief system behind what was being suggested as the "right" way to create their resume. Many of the examples given were downright terrible in my opinion. Worse yet, if followed, the examples could have hurt my clients in many cases.

Most publications then tell you what to do. They will say use action verbs, and then present an expanded list of action verbs. Often the examples are presented in past tense (supervised, delegated) rather than the strongest verb form, which is present tense with an -ing (supervising, delegating). The active voice (supervising, delegating) projects the client as young, active, alert, vibrant, excited and ready to get on with it. The passive tense (supervised, delegated) is more like past tense, dull and never was.

This strikes me as pretty simple stuff, and yet I have never seen it presented in any book about resume writing. I find that much of the advice I give my clients is about 180 degrees from what is offered in the marketplace and on the bookshelves today. Clearly, the more knowledge and understanding you have of the marketplace today, the quicker you are going to navigate your way though it.

After cogitating on these observations, I have come to the conclusion that *many books tell you what to do, but do not really share with you how to do it. Nor do they always tell you why to do it a certain way.* This book is an effort to help correct that deficiency.

Understanding that there really isn't a right or wrong answer for many of the tasks involved in marketing yourself and writing a resume, this effort is then a result of my judgment. Yours may differ. Perhaps a different opinion may spur discussion in the public arena. Discussion is certainly not going to eliminate the truth, but it may help better define and identify the truth we know and accept.

You can give me feedback at http://quality-resumes-by-ed-bagley.com

Ed Bagley

Lacey, WA
4-20-12

Index

Part 1

Personal Marketing - Your Key to Getting Ahead

Personal marketing is the phrase I use to describe repositioning yourself in the economy following a merger, acquisition, restructuring or downsizing.

A potential hire generally thinks about writing a resume or updating his or her resume in preparation for the job hunt ahead. The first request they can expect to get is for an email resume to be posted online at a job search site or in response to an organization's online application.

This book is not about how to create or post an email resume online – that subject is plenty complicated enough for another email report. This book is also not on where to look for your next job, another extensive subject for another book.

This book focuses on a necessary starting point for anyone looking for a job: **How to Write a Single Page Resume.** If the position you are attempting to secure pays $40,000 or less, then a single page product will work in most cases. So, let's begin at the beginning: Personal marketing starts with asking some very basic questions.

When I first interview a potential client, I might say to them: When I chatted with you on the phone, I can't remember if I asked you if you are working now or not. Then I shut up and listen to the client's reply.

Normally he or she will reply that, yes, they are working now, no, they are not, or they are in between.

If they tell me it's ABC Company they are working for, but don't volunteer their position, I will follow with: What are you doing for ABC Company?

Next, I want to know how long they have been with the company or organization, and how long they have been in their current or most recent career field.

Other questions I am likely to ask include:

Where are you educationally? (In other words, do you have any college degrees, and what are they).

Other than your formal education, have you ever been to a voc-tech school or college for any training and certification? (I want to know about technical or specialized training.)

Have you ever been active duty military?

What are you thinking you want to do now? (They didn't come to me because they were interested in keeping their job, with the possible exception of being made to reapply for the position they already have during a merger, acquisition, restructuring or downsizing.)

What kind of income do you want to generate? (How much money do you want to make.)

All of these questions are very important in giving me a good picture of what the client's present position is in the current market.

If you are going to help market a client, you had better know what they have to offer a potential employer.

When I do a single page resume for a client, I identify the client and where to find him or her, and then develop an objective.

Your Objective Is Your Business Card

I believe the objective you put on a resume is very important for four reasons:

First, other than your name and address, it should be the first thing the potential employer reads, and therefore must be short and impressive.

Second, it's easy to forget that people hiring have needs, and one of their first questions is: Does your want fill my need?

7

Third, it doesn't pay in this (2012) economy to be what I call a wandering generality; it does pay to be a meaningful specific (that is, to have the education, training and/or experience to offer).

Fourth, companies will pay for some training in a good economy, but in a down economy like The Great Recession currently ongoing, they do not want to pay a dime for training. They want you to hit down running when you are hired, and already know what you are doing.

About 60% of the clients I deal with don't have an objective like a single rifle bullet. They don't normally come to me and say: I want to be a doctor; I'll pay the price, whatever it takes.

They tend to be people who, like many of you, have enough life experience and job experience to be capable of doing many different kinds of things.

A lot of people graduate with a teaching degree, can't find employment as a teacher, eventually take a job selling insurance, and then never leave the insurance business for 30 years.

It doesn't mean they are not capable of doing many other jobs; it just means that they got stuck earning an income and never left the security for another opportunity.

What I do in all cases is to gather a lot of information about the client, and then give them some direction from a marketing standpoint. I want to capture the resume reader by nailing down the objective clearly, concisely and impressively. Having done so, the probability of the reader continuing to read the resume is almost 100% if I'm creating the resume product.

I've talked about personal marketing being so important in this (2012) economy. Let's digress a moment and examine why that is so in Part 2.

Part 2

There Are More Qualified People Chasing Fewer Good Positions

Finding a "good" job in the near future will be more difficult than easy because there really are more aspiring workers available than positions for them to fill.

There have been very few times in recent years when those hiring have had to go out the front door and bring in the most likely looking prospects for employment. Just the opposite has been true. Those hiring have had the time to pick and choose among the best talent and most qualified candidates available.

The Conditions That Shaped Today's Marketplace and Hiring Practices

The current challenge in getting hired arises from many market conditions. Some factors are:

1) Most of us genuinely want to get ahead, so we look for opportunities to increase our wages and benefits when we are both employed and unemployed. Thus, your competition for employment is both those already employed and those seeking employment.

2) All potential employers are subject to general economic conditions as employers and consequently tend to put a freeze on hiring or reduce staffing in a slow growing or stagnant economy.

3) Improvements in equipment and systems have reduced some opportunities to get your foot in the door; the effect of technology in our world and economy has been rapid and, at times, overwhelming, giving rise to what has been called the "Second Economy" (the rise of technology which increases productivity and replaces people).

4) The force and effect of the union movement has been diminished in recent years, and companies seem more willing to shut down businesses or operations rather than fuss with unions over wage and benefit concessions.

5) Colleges and universities keep trying to meet the demand of students to acquire a degree, and students keep charging through school without, in some cases, any meaningful regard for the lack of demand in specific job markets.

6) Companies began to realize that their products or services were not as competitive as they had thought, and that their lack of productivity limited their growth and profitability, causing investors to look at better opportunities to invest their money.

7) The lack of productivity helped lead to massive layoffs and cutbacks in corporate personnel especially, giving companies more efficiency, more productivity, more liquidity and more investors with the prospect of a higher return on their investment.

8) Pure greed with lying, cheating and stealing by corporate leaders at huge banks and financial lenders led to a crash in the housing market unseen since the Great Depression. A corresponding crash among the companies responsible for The Great Recession led to a rescue by government financing at the taxpayer's expense. It was and has been devastating to millions of workers since it started in mid-2007.

Despite prevailing factors in the current economy, employment attitudes tend to be relative to a person's individual situation. It doesn't really matter how much your government tells you things are great and getting better if you are broke and unemployed.

Conversely, the economy can be lousy, but if you are among those successfully employed and making good money, you are not nearly so concerned about the employment situation.

Compensation also tends to be relative to the individual. A person making $3,000 a month is doing great compared to a person who is broke and unemployed. However, a person making $10,000 a month figures the person making $3,000 a month is doing lousy.

The Difference Between a Job and an Opportunity

Before I proceed further, let's get this comment out: Getting a job is not that big of a deal. Some unemployed workers do not want to hear what I just said, but let's stop playing games and face the truth: There are literally thousands of job opportunities that go begging for a worker every day. The signs are in storefront windows everywhere.

When some unemployed workers say there are no jobs, what they literally mean is: There are no jobs at $20.00 an hour doing what I want to do when I want to do it.

The problem is most workers do not want to work 1) for a minimum wage, 2) doing something they do not want to do, 3) for someone they do not want to do it for, 4) at a time when they don't want to do it. I wouldn't want to either, but that does not mean there are no jobs available.

Working a crummy job for minimum wage on the graveyard shift is not very appealing, and it is even less so for a recent college graduate who envisioned a good paying job with good conditions and interesting work. What most of us are looking for is a position that offers job satisfaction with good wages and benefits, an extensive training program, and a chance for advancement.

There is a world of difference between the two opportunities. To summarize: Getting a job is no big deal; finding a "good" opportunity is a big deal in terms of satisfaction, income, benefits, training and potential for advancement. Only 1 in 50 prospects will actually land a "good" position using common methods of job hunting. This percentage is unacceptable unless you are the 1 in 50. The purpose of this book is to share with you why it pays to listen, offer some insight about hiring practices, share some techniques which can increase your chances of success in getting hired, and share with you how to write an excellent resume.

I do not guarantee that what I share with you will cause you to get hired (how could I; I am not doing the hiring); however, what I share with you has worked well for hundreds of my clients, and there is no reason why, on the face of it, to think that these suggestions and methods will not work for you.

I want to **help you become successful** as a client; I do not want any part of failure.

Part 3

Millions of Workers Are Unemployed or Underemployed

How the World Has Changed

One of the most common approaches to getting hired in the past was to march into a place, ask for an application, fill it out, turn it in and hope that someone, somewhere will answer that, yes, we have a position open, and you, among the many, have been selected for the job.

The odds of this happening today are very long indeed if you are looking for a "good" opportunity and not a minimum wage job.

First, employers do not give out hard copy applications for you to fill out anymore. If you are filling out an application, it is going to be online on the Internet. Today you post your email resume online, and you fill out job applications online.

Businesses and organizations do not want you crashing their door, bothering them about potential employment, forcing them to hire more personnel to deal with you while taking time away from their production to handle your job queries.

If most businesses advertised for a "good" position today and said come by at 8 a.m. Monday to fill out an application, they could have hundreds of applicants early Monday morning and a possible riot to deal with as applicants pushed and jockeyed for position in line.

Unanticipated and Overwhelming Response

The business attitude on entertaining employment prospects face-to-face, or even over the phone, is rooted in the reality of what happened to Boeing some 16 years ago.

11

Consider this: In February, 1996, Boeing placed full page ads in Sunday papers throughout the Puget Sound Area in Washington (the state on the West Coast). Boeing, an aircraft manufacturer, invited those without Boeing experience to consider becoming assembly mechanics and gave a hot line number to call the following morning.

By day's end, Boeing received 77,024 calls to 8 operators with a system that was designed to handle only 53 callers simultaneously. Imagine what would have happened if Boeing said, come on down to the plant and apply!

Today, Boeing, which used to accept hard copy applications for employment in positions that were currently open, and then dumped the hard copy application process and went to resumes only, now makes all potential employees send an email resume that is not an attachment to an email. This means the email resume has to literally go into the body of their online application so that no viruses come into their system via an attachment. Yes, it is a different world today for any worker who has been around the block once or twice.

Second, it's possible to walk into a business today and ask about employment opportunities, and be told that they are not hiring at the present time, when, in fact, they are in the process of hiring three people through their online hiring system. They would screen the online applications, select candidates to interview and hire, and you would never know the difference. The bottom line is that they are not going to spend their time educating you on how the world communicates today. If you do not know, and are not willing to learn on your own, you will be left out of the process, and out of a potential job.

It is rare today for a business to advertise in the newspaper and ask you to send in a hard copy of your resume. When they do, you should be overjoyed and respond immediately with your hard copy resume and cover letter. Many times you may find yourself mailing your resume to what is really a blind post office box number; often you have no idea which business it is, or what opportunity it is to which you are responding. Do it anyway.

Third, I advise clients never to fill out hard copy applications, and only online applications when you can easily cut and paste the resume in one function. I do not want my clients filling out applications that are compartmentalized (a box for each request) because it takes too much time, and allows the job website or company to build a database with your personal information that they can and do sell. Sometimes they will have a box to cut and paste for your resume, and another box for your cover letter, however, avoid the compartmentalized collection sites like the plague.

While it is illegal to ask you your age, a business can legally ask you your salary history, how much you want to make, reasons why you left jobs, your medical history, and specific references. This information alone is worth much to a business but can **only hurt you**, the client, 100 out of 100 times.

Resumes I generate contain none of the aforementioned information. This information is simply not appropriate at the resume stage; it is more appropriate at the interview stage; however, even at the interview stage it is not appropriate unless they demonstrate an indicated interest in you as a prospect, and you, in turn, are genuinely interested in the opportunity.

Information That Can Damage Your Chances

I do not use age because it seems we are always too young or too old for the job. This is an especially painful topic for anyone just graduating from high school, or retiring from their first career but not ready to stop working.

I do not use your salary history or what you want to make because this automatically prices you into or out of the opportunity. You do not want to price yourself out of an opportunity by giving a figure too high, or settle for less than what it is you have to offer by giving a figure too low.

The time to talk about compensation is at the end of the interview when you have all but been hired, not in your online application or resume product up front.

I do not talk about why you left a position in an online application. Simply say, "Better Opportunity". Let them assume the best, that you are upward mobile and want to switch positions for more job satisfaction, more opportunity, more pay and more benefits.

I do not mention specific references in the resume because, if someone can read your resume, check your references, and--on that basis--make a decision not to interview you or hire you, you have done yourself a great disservice. You want to get in front of people, eyeball to eyeball, using the force of your personality and verbal skills to sell yourself as the candidate to hire.

Why You Should Hire a Professional Resume Writer

Most of us are far better verbally than we think we are. We spend most of our lives talking, not writing. It is in the area of written skills that most of us do not fare nearly as well.

Even if we learn how to write going through school, and are literate, we tend to lose what we do not use over a period of time. You may be able to write the great American novel, or technical journals, or business memos, but if you have not been writing resumes day in and day out and learning in the process, it does not much matter that you can do other kinds of writing. Resume writing is a very specific kind of writing; and just because one can write excellent resumes does not mean that same person can write the great American novel.

Most of us are required to talk on our job every day; few of us are required to write resume products every day we are on the job.

Again, to summarize, Quality-Resumes-by-Ed-Bagley.com suggests that you avoid filling out applications like the plague. Unfortunately, if you are applying for public service positions (working for the local, state or federal government, for example), you will not have a choice; you will probably have to fill out an application to get hired.

Ditto for workers who are in teaching, law enforcement, fire protection and city or county organizations.

Businesses, in contrast, generally prefer resumes to applications when considering candidates for "good" (that is, more responsible and better paying) opportunities.

Why Some Qualified People Do Not Get Hired

There are basically two reasons why some qualified candidates do not get hired.

One, they simply are not out beating the bushes, hitting the bricks and stirring the pot to cause something good to happen. Employers are not going to come to your doorstep. You have to create friction by separating the seat of your pants from the easy chair and get moving with concrete, positive action toward your goal: getting hired.

Two, for those who are out trying to make something happen, they cannot secure interviews.

The single biggest reason why they are not securing interviews is the online application they are filling out --for the reasons discussed earlier--or the hard copy resume product they are using.

Most clients develop a mental attitude that focuses on finding a job when they would be better served to adopt a thought process and mental attitude that focuses on securing interviews.

How many people are hired who are not first interviewed? The interview almost always precedes the hiring process and therefore should get most of your attention. Stop looking for a job; start trying to secure interviews. Consider informational interviews with an employer if you cannot secure job interviews. Informational interviews allow you to merely find out about what an industry or a specific job is like, and if you might be interested in considering a career in that vocation. If you can secure interviews, you are probably going to get job offers sooner or later.

You do need, when interviewing, to look, act and talk effectively: three conditions that can be improved with awareness and practice.

14

Part 4

Why It Pays to Listen

If you have been using common methods to gain employment and have not been successful, you need to change your methods.

If you keep applying the same methods you have been using, you will be no further ahead one year from today than you are now. If the shoe fits, wear it. We have two ears and one mouth, yet seldom do we listen twice as much as we talk. What I am about to share with you may secure you a good opportunity if you listen and apply the ideas discussed.

The Importance of Your Resume Product

The use of online or hard copy resumes in the hiring process today has become commonplace to employers advertising and prospects looking for jobs.

Years ago people would simply fill out an application or send in a resume and wait for a call to interview, or follow up with the employer if they did not get a call. If the effort failed, they repeated the process until they were hired. Many potential employees--especially those in sales--would talk their way past a receptionist or secretary and into an interview with the boss. Both of these methods seldom, if ever, work any more in finding "good" opportunities.

The One Constant is Change

It is a changing world in the hiring process. The concept of using an email resume approach to hiring has exploded nationally, and I predict it will become a necessity in the future for finding "good" employment opportunities.

That said, always have an excellent hard copy resume and cover letter to take with you when you are called for an interview. Recognize that interviews are seldom one-to-one anymore. Now it tends to be to be one to a committee of interviewers.

When the interviewers are reading your online application and trying to interview you at the same time, which is tacky and they do it all the time, immediately get up and give each of them hard copies of your resume and cover letter. It is the hard copy that sells you best, and puts your best foot forward. The online application contains the same information, but the online application has zero style points for presentation and impact. This is especially true if you have been able to cut and paste a copy of your hard copy resume and cover letter, rather than having to fill out a compartmentalized form block by block.

When my clients are forced to fill out an application one block at a time, I recommend that they use the resume I generate for them as a resource document in filling out the application.

When you can turn in your online application by hand, don't ask if they want your hard copy resume and cover letter with the application; include it with the application when you turn it in. Never ask because it invites a yes/no answer, and if their answer is no, you are dead in the water.

It's Only Your Future

If you have to fill out a hard copy application (almost unheard of today), don't do it in the office because it puts you under pressure to do it immediately. It is too easy to forget important information, or regret what you said or how you said it when you have more time to think about what you wrote *after* you have turned in your application.

Ask for two copies of the application if you must fill one out. Tell them you need one to get everything important down and will use the second one to prepare a nice, neat copy for them.

If they will not give you two copies, always make another copy so you can put things down first without messing up the original. We are not talking about anything important here, just your future. You want to save time and irritation in filling out more applications.

Think about a potential employer advertising for a position and asking for your email resume. They normally have hundreds of resumes to read when trying to determine whom to interview. Large corporations can get hundreds of email applications or cut and paste resumes daily in response to job offerings.

If you do not think how your resume is received is important, think about this: You are not there to sell yourself when they read it. Your resume had better sing and dance compared to the many others they are reading because it is on this basis that they are deciding whom to interview and whom not to interview. Remember, no interview, no job.

Why First Impressions Are Important

Unfortunately, your first opportunity to impress may also happen to be your last as well as your only opportunity. There may, of course, be other opportunities. While I would agree that it is not good to judge a book by its cover, this is exactly what is happening to you when you submit your resume. Your resume is your book cover. We know that everything that really counts comes from inside of us; that we can't really judge people accurately by external observations, such as our looks, color or race.

16

We can't measure determination, heart or desire because it comes from within.

It's like motivation; motivation is an "inside" job. This is why the employer can't tell exactly how you will work out on the job until you are asked to perform.

The Idea Is to Get Attention

As much as I would like to tell you differently, the number one job your resume has to do first is to get attention.

A lot of clients correctly assume the idea of the resume is to get attention, but if it were that easy, I could put your hard copy resume on lime green paper with sequins as a border, and it would get attention! It would go up on the wall at the personnel office and be the best joke in the office for months; employees would fall off their chairs laughing. This is what I call negative attention.

What you need is positive attention. Your hard copy resume must be conservative, understated and tasteful; the equivalent of a three-piece suit, boardroom and status; the essence of banking and finance.

If it does not get attention and hence read seriously, it doesn't really matter how much education or experience you have to offer. No one will read far enough to notice.

Copying your resume on 20-pound, white bond paper is not going to cut the mustard, even though you may be trying to save money in the process. You're not in a contest here to see who is the most frugal.

Save money for the company after you are hired; never spare any cost in promoting yourself first. You can save cents or even dollars in promoting yourself, and lose thousands of dollars in the process.

I recommend putting your resume on colored paper that has a light, subtle hue, such as ivory or a light gray. Avoid dark colors of any hue; stay away from pink, green, yellow and blue. It's not that other colors of paper won't work. In fact, they will. It is recognizing that they work a percentage of the time, as do the light, subtle hues I am recommending. What we are trying to figure out here is: Which colors work with the most employers the most amount of time?

Use a better grade of paper than 20 pound bond; try 24 pound parchtone, for example, which is really 60 pound book stock quality. I personally use an ivory paper on 80-pound stock for a single page resume. Use envelopes that match the color of your resume. If you write a cover letter--and I highly recommend that you do--have the cover letter to match also. To summarize: **Always be a class act in this area; never be cheap.**

You do not have to literally have your resume printed by a print shop. If you are using a good word processor, or computer with a laser printer, your product can be copied on a copy machine and look good.

Part 5

The Two Key Factors in Writing a Resume

I don't believe there is a "right" and a "wrong" way to write a resume.

For example: Let's say you and I knew each other and graduated from high school together. You write your resume and then find out that I'm now in the resume writing business. You come to see me, and here is what you say: "Ed, good to see you. I wrote my own resume and found out you're in the biz. Here it is, what do you think?"

Regardless of how well or how terrible your effort may be, I'm not likely to say, "This is not how we do it now, but this is (and then point to a resume I have produced)."

The fact is, when you write your own resume, it would still contain a lot of "what we say" about you if someone takes the time and trouble to read it.

When you decide that you want me to do it for you, then, **more important than what we say will be how we say what we say.**

Now I'm talking about experience, expertise, language skill, knowing what to say, what not to say, and why.

For the purpose of this book, I am going to share three very important things with you:

One, the secrets of personal marketing.

Two, the secrets of how to write a quality resume.

Three, how the two elements--personal marketing and writing a quality resume—can go together to create posture, and a viable presentation in marketing yourself.

There are several ways to write resumes that have proven effective in getting hired. I believe that even a terrible resume, by professional standards, can work; if you circulate enough copies, someone, somewhere at sometime will likely respond to it.

Usually it's just a matter of how long it will take to get a response.

How to Get Where You Want to Go Faster

When you have a professional writer like me do it, I simply reduce the amount of time it takes for you to get where you want to go.

To summarize: **Always remember that almost anything will work a percentage of the time. What we are trying to figure out is: which presentation works with the most employers the most amount of time.**

While it's good that, as a professional writer, that I have a college degree in journalism, have an ability to write, and am literate, I really believe that the two most important factors in crafting resume products are judgment and taste.

The Most Important Factor in Writing Resumes

Judgment is the most important factor in writing a resume, and--as you know--we cannot teach people judgment. We get judgment from life experience, and what experience shows us is that some people simply have better judgment than others.

I can show you men who keep running into brick walls because they have not figured out how to climb over them, walk around them, dig under them, or blow them up and walk through. That is a lack of judgment.

If you are a parent, this is what I mean: We raise our children to have a sense of right and wrong, and to make good decisions when it counts. But try as we might, there comes that day and time when we are not there, and someone offers them cigarettes, or drugs, or something worse.

At that point in time, we hope and pray that our child makes the right decision because the wrong decision might lead them down a road from which they may never return. That is judgment. They cannot get it by you simply telling them what to do or not to do; they also need modeling, the power of whatever influence you may have with them, and osmosis, the experience of making judgments, failing, and making better judgments.

Judgment is the most critical factor you are going to have to come to terms with in writing a resume; or judgment may be your most telling weakness when you go to the street to test its effectiveness.

The Second Most Important Factor

Taste is the second most important factor in writing a resume and has an important role to play as well. By taste I mean the initial impression, the color of the paper, the kind of type, the format and the choice of words. There is power in words; we can say things positively, negatively or neutrally: our choice of words can work for or against us.

I am a professional writer, but I am also a farmer in the sense that, when I write, I plant seeds in the product calculated to do one of two things:

First, create mental images.

Second, move people to the action we want them to take.

And I suggest that there is only one action that counts, and that is the action of the employer picking up the phone to call you for an interview.

Both of these factors--judgment and taste--are very subjective in nature; that would be true no matter with whom you dealt.

I think these factors are so subjective that it's difficult for someone to pick up a resume product I did and say, "Objectively, on a scale of 1 to 10, we'll give Ed a 9 for this fine effort."

Anyone could pick up a resume product I did and say it's a piece of crap; that would be their opinion. The salient factor is: does it work? And by work, I mean secure interviews for the client.

How to Know If Your Resume Is Effective

The test for effectiveness for a resume is not whether you secure a job; the test is whether you secure interviews. I have hundreds of clients with responsible, good paying positions that put my products to work and may secure 5 interviews, get 5 offers and accept none of them.

This happens frequently because the offer they receive is not really that much better than the position and compensation they currently have, especially if it involves moving to another location.

An executive who is offered another $10,000 in annual salary and must move to take advantage of the opportunity may be well advised to refuse the opportunity. Even if the company making the offer pays for the moving expenses, there are numerous nickel and dime expenses in moving yourself or your family that are not anticipated.

You have to calculate not only the actual dollars and cents issues, but also the impact on yourself and your family if you move. You may be well liked and respected where you are employed and in no danger of losing your position in the near term.

You also have no guarantee--if you take the offer and move--that you are going to like the new opportunity and compensation any better once you get acclimated to new digs and responsibilities.

20

If married, your spouse and children will likely be leaving family, friends and schoolmates behind, with the prospect of going it alone until they meet and make new friends in a new environment.

The Cheapest Commodity in the World

Always remember that the cheapest commodity in the world is opinions. Everyone has one, and if you do not think so, just ask them; they will tell you.

I recommend that you ask a lot of questions and even solicit opinions, but I urge you to be careful about from whom you take your advice.

Some clients making $100,000+ a year get pushed out the door during a merger, acquisition, restructuring or downsizing (all words for the same negative impact on the individual involved), head down to the local watering hole, ask some unemployed, broke person for advice on what to do now, and then actually listen as if the unemployed, broke person could tell them how to be successful in life.

And yet this habit goes on all the time. The sources of advice are all around us: fellow employees, those who did not get axed, other friends, your relative who has never had a job, your pastor, and, if you are desperate enough, your dog Spot.

When you want advice, never go back down the ladder, always climb higher until you reach someone more successful or accomplished than you are in a certain area. Let someone with proven experience, expertise and success suggest meaningful actions that can actually produce potential results.

Always remember that when you take advice from anyone, 999 times out of a 1,000, they are not going to hire you. Nor are you hiring yourself, so what you think counts for little.

Why Marketing and Probability Are Important

In addition to judgment and taste, there are two other elements that I deem important to success in the job-hunting process. They are marketing and probability.

Marketing is important because if you do not know where you are going, you might not like where you wind up. You need to figure out your niche in the market--what your skills are, what knowledge you have, and where you would like to put it to use.

I tell clients that while I know on most days their body temperatures are 98.6, they also represent to me a 6-pack of Coca-Cola Classic. My job, from a marketing standpoint, is to take that 6-pack (my client) from my desk to the shelves of a supermarket (the employer).

Getting the 6-pack into the supermarket is "marketing" for me; after it is there and we build an end-aisle display and blow it out for 79 cents on Super Bowl Weekend, that is "merchandising" that leads to a sale.

Probability, the second element, simply suggests that there is not an absolutely correct approach or method to getting hired. It is more a matter of trying to figure out what works most often with the most potential employers.

Never Underestimate the Power of Probability

There is absolutely no question, however, that if we do certain things one way rather than another, that it can, in fact, increase the probability of something good happening.

I am absolutely not in the theory business. I do not do anything for a client and hope it will work. I am in the results business. I do for clients what I have already done for clients in the same approximate position that has worked--real world, real time--and when we do things this way, with the benefit of feedback of clients, the probability of something good happening rises dramatically.

The important thing for you is to follow--to the best of your ability--the information I am going to be sharing with you about personal marketing and writing resumes.

I am a personal marketing consultant and a professional writer with more than 50 years of experience who has helped literally thousands of people get to where they want to go.

Part 6

The Single Page Resume and Why It Works for Lower Incomes

For the purpose of my presentation here, I am going to concentrate on sharing with you how to write a successful one page resume.

You should know that the single page resume is the most common resume product. My experience shows it works really well for positions up to approximately $40,000 in annual income, or roughly $3,300 a month, or roughly $20 an hour. This is especially true if you are just trying to get your foot in the door. Another reason why the single page resume is so popular is that there are a lot more people earning less than $40,000 a year than there are people earning more than $40,000 a year.

If you are an executive or professional person with an annual income of $50,000 and up (normally $50,000 to $80,000 for most people) and are interested in management or supervision, then brochure products will work much better than a single page resume.

Brochure products I design are printed on 11-by-17-inch paper (which folded equals a 4-page brochure that really is a 2-page resume with a full cover page, or a 3-page resume with a full cover page), or are printed on 11-by-14-inch paper (which folded equals a 2-and-a-half page resume with a split cover).

For the purpose of sharing information here, my remarks will refer to writing a single page resume; however, everything I say can and should be used to write a more upscale, brochure product for executives and professionals as well.

The Main Purpose of a Resume

The **main purpose** of your resume product is to secure interviews. You should know that the concept and approach I share with you regarding a single page resume has worked very well for hundreds of clients, and there is no reason to think it will not work for you.

The **second purpose** of your resume product is to establish your qualifications so, when you go into an interview, their purpose is not to fuss with you about whether you can do the job.

When they call you to interview, the odds say they have already decided you can basically do the job, or you are capable of learning the job.

The Really Key Questions That Concern Employers

Their intent is usually to check out your personality. They ask themselves questions like:

What kind of a person are you?

Will you be able to get along with members of our staff?

Will you bring customers to us or drive them away from us, depending upon how you treat people?

The probability of this single page resume working for you is good because we are going to accomplish three things in the writing process.

First, we are going to build posture into the language.

Second, we are going to show an ability to deal with people at every possible turn.

Third, we are going to identify leadership ability at every level relative to peer group if it is there.

Too many potential employees come through the front door of a business and their poor mental attitude precedes them. They come hat in hand, projecting an attitude that says, "I need a job. Please hire me." This is not posture.

Learn to adopt an attitude that projects you as an "arm's length professional". That is: You have skills to offer and goals and objectives to accomplish. You are not entertaining any discussion about whether you will attain your goals and objectives; it is simply a matter of which company or organization you are going to help in attaining your goals and objectives.

If the company **is** interested, then I say, "Fantastic, let's talk."

If the company **is not** interested, I say, "Fantastic, let's talk to someone else."

As difficult as it may be, **you must learn to not take rejection personally and understand that you will not relate the same to everyone.**

The best sales reps in the world don't suffer a paralysis of analysis when they face rejection. They don't feel sorry for themselves, whine or complain. When people don't buy, they don't ask what's wrong with their product, what's wrong with themselves, or what's wrong the company, or person who didn't buy. They don't attempt to explain what happened by a confluence of the stars or the morning horoscope for their birth sign. **They simply knock on another door.**

They recognize that they are not going to relate to everybody, and they are not hung up on it.

I tell clients that for every 10 people who could potentially make the decision to interview you or hire you, 3 out of the 10 will like you, and it will have nothing to do with what you do. They may simply **like** your smile, your handshake, the sound of your voice, or the way you part your hair.

Rest assured that 3 out of those same 10 people will not like you, and again it will have nothing to do with what you do. They may simply **not like** your smile, your handshake, the sound of your voice or the way you part your hair.

Four out of those same 10 people will learn to like you or dislike you as they develop a working relationship with you.

The odds say that those 4 in 10 will like you if you work at earning their respect, honor their confidence, and treat them as you would want to be treated.

Considering these numbers, you should be able to develop a very good working relationship with about 70% of your fellow employees when you are hired and go to work.

The other 30% you can forget, and if you bend over backwards to cultivate their good will, you will usually find that they always have a reason to whine or complain about what's happening to them, and why the world isn't treating them right. They are, in a word, negative.

Your best positive will not likely overcome their negative. So forget about them, or they may do mental harm to your psyche.

What Can Explain This Phenomenon?

Why do people like or not like you based upon things that really have little to do with your skills and abilities?

The answer is simply that people are not always rational. People are filled up with prejudices, beliefs, foibles and idiosyncrasies. They will continually tell you that cat is spelled "kat" even though you would lead them to a dictionary and show them that cat is spelled "cat".

A **man** convinced against his will is of the same opinion still.
A **woman** convinced against her will is of the same opinion still.

Under the category of "people are not always rational" is also the phenomenon of "life is not always fair".

For those of us who have been paying attention, life is not fair, and it is not just an occasional circumstance that arises.

A good example of this would be a client named Karen who went to a job interview, had a fantastic experience at the interview, came away feeling good about herself and her prospects of being hired.

She knew that the company representatives liked her and would offer her a job. She did not get the offer.

Later she learned that everyone liked her, but the key decision-maker axed her hiring, even though he seemed to have liked her at the interview.

What Karen did not know was that the key decision-maker was going through a nasty divorce and child custody battle, and his ex-wife's name was Karen. He simply did not want to come to work every day and have to smile at this Karen and say, "Good morning, Karen, how are you doing?" Such is life.

25

Too many potential hires spend too much time trying to pursue one particular opportunity rather than pursuing many possible opportunities. Learn that there are many opportunities available to be filled and that **you are just the right person** to fill one of them.

Remember, if they are interested and want to talk to you, fantastic, let's talk; if they are not interested, fantastic, let's talk to someone else.

Part 7

The Elements of a Single Page Resume

First, let me make it absolutely clear that I do not believe there is a right or wrong way to do this resume writing process. My approach, or your approach, has to do with two important factors: judgment and taste.

When I say there are eight basic elements involved in creating a resume product, this is **my judgment only** since there is no definitive answer to the question: How many elements should we use?

I believe there are eight basic elements in creating a single page resume product. Certainly there are many others that could be added or covered as well, but remember, we are creating a single page resume, not writing a book.

The eight elements are: 1) The Heading, 2) The Objective, 3) A Summary of Qualifications, 4) Educational Background, 5) Specialized Training, 6) Professional Highlights, 7) Military Background, and 8) Personal Data. These elements do not necessarily have to appear in the order in which I am listing them; much has to do with what information you have to offer within each element. Information can change the order of some elements in a heartbeat since **we are seeking to influence with words and will give the most ink to the most important, or best, information.**

Let's get started by sharing with you not just **what** to do in writing resumes, but **how** to do it. You can find an example of a single page resume and cover letter on pages 70 and 71, and refer to it as we go through the resume writing process. Don't miss the important notes about the resume and cover letter examples on pages 72 and 73.

Always Put Your Name First

Your first consideration is The Heading. Many clients want to start by putting "RESUME" at the top of the page. I highly recommend that you do not do this.

I have found that people reading these resume products are generally bright people; they easily recognize a resume when they see one.

If you would want the potential employer to remember one thing about you, what would it be? Your name, of course. Always put your name first at the top of the page. I recommend you do it in bold face, all capitals, and put two spaces between your first name and your last name. Using your middle name or initial is a waste of time and space. It simple draws attention away from your last name, which **IS** what you want them to remember.

Skip a line and then put a continuous line underneath leading over to the words "professional profile" in bold face, lower case type flush right.

Skip another line and then put your complete address flush right on one line, your city, state and zip code flush right on the next line, and finally your area code and telephone number flush right on the last line. I do not recommend using your email address because personnel types are voiceless, faceless and hide behind emails in the hiring process. You want people to call you so you can gather valuable field information from their voice and attitude over the phone that can be critical in the hiring process.

Then leave a line of space before your objective. It should look like this:

ED BAGLEY
_____**professional profile**

P. O. Box 3658
Lacey, WA 98509
Telephone: (253) 000-0000

Two added notes of importance:

First, understand that while these how-to directions are exacting in nature and provide you a detailed road map of where and how to tackle the next element, remember again that in my opinion there is no right or wrong way to write resumes. Everything I suggest is a matter of style (not right and wrong), and is based on judgment and taste. That said, it works very well and I have the results to prove it.

Second, names are important and we should treat them with importance because potential employers can react to names. For example, if your last name is unusual, difficult to spell or pronounce, it is even more important that you drop your middle name or initial. Smith, Jones and Brown are common as common can be. DeGregorio, Sogge and Nicholyavich are not.

My thinking behind dropping your middle name or initial is that you want the person hiring you to remember DeGregorio, for example; your middle name or initial merely takes attention away from your last name.

If your last name is unusual, difficult to spell or pronounce, you are going to be more marketable with just your first name and last name only.

Another consideration is that DeGregorio, for example, is five syllables. If the first name was Ann, the first name would be one syllable and the last name would be five syllables. One syllable moves more quickly to dealing with the last name and staying there longer, which is important since the last name has five syllables.

How You Say Your Name Can Be Important

If your last name is unusual, difficult to spell or pronounce, I also recommend that the third thing you do when you interview, after smiling and sticking out your hand, is to downshift from third to first gear when saying your name; in other words, say your name slowly and draw attention to it.

For example, "My name is Ann DeGregorio.. My last name is Italian, has five syllables, and can be difficult to spell and pronounce. It's pronounced, De-Gre-gor-ri-o, but everyone calls me Ann and you can too."

When you invite them to call you by your easy to pronounce first name, you eliminate the need for them to fuss with your last name. Like computer software, you instantly become user friendly and more likeable, not to mention savvy in public relations and marketing.

This is a very thoughtful thing to do because many immigrants have names that are not easy to pronounce correctly the first time around. Expecting an interviewer to pronounce your name correctly when it is difficult to do so is just plain stupid, and shows how unaware you are about people skills.

This can be extremely important to you, since, if the interviewer does not catch your name up front, or is uncomfortable pronouncing it, he or she may not use your name while addressing you during the interview, and this can be a disaster.

Clearly, the more times the interviewer uses your name, the better chance you have of being remembered in a positive way. You should also know that the more times an interviewer addresses you by your name in the interview, the more likely you are to get a job offer.

Another name consideration that is a little, but important nuance, involves your first name.

28

If your first name, for example, is Robert and you are an outside sales representative, it may--from a marketing standpoint--make a whole lot of sense to use Bob or Rob rather than Robert. **Robert** is formal; **Bob** is less formal, but really, isn't this the image you should try to project?

You want to be someone who is not pretentious, but easygoing and friendly, someone who is not intimidating or demanding, but, who, if asked a question, would respond while sending out positive feelings.

If your name is Robert, and you're in sales and you need to relate to people, ask yourself this question: How many of the adult males you work with call you Robert? Chances are good that everyone calls you Bob except your mother, and she only calls you Robert when she's upset with you.

On the other hand, if I had a client (I don't) named **T. Brice Wadcalader III** who wanted to be a mortgage banker, I might say to him, "T. Brice, we wouldn't want to change your name at all." Doesn't T. Brice Wadcalader III sound like a snooty banker? It does to me, and I'll bet it does to others as well.

A special note to women who are executives and professionals: If you use your first and middle name with your last name, be careful. A good example would be Betty Sue Rawlings.

If you are my client, I immediately suggest we drop the middle name. Betty Sue is just not going to fly as well in the corporate boardroom.

Women who use their first and middle names, like Betty Sue or Sally Mae, tend to sound less professional. The same is true for men who are Billy Ray. Mary Lou Retton can get away with it, but how many gold medals have you won?

Now don't get mad at me. I didn't say this was rational or right; I said you need to *sound more professional.*

Occasionally, women can drop the names and use their initials only, but be careful. Betty Sue Rawlings becomes B. S. Rawlings, and I think the problem here is obvious. She would be much more marketable as Betty Rawlings.

I recognize that women, like men, are going to do what they are going to do; however, being liberated is not necessarily synonymous with being street smart. And, whether women like it or not, there still is a glass ceiling to the boardroom.

Why not do what works better, and then change the corporate culture when you reach the top? Remember, my job is to help you succeed; that means recognizing the turf and developing a game plan that has the best chance of immediate success.

Part 8

An Objective Gives Your Direction

Your second consideration is The Objective. From this point forward, refer to the sample single page resume and cover letter examples on pages 70 and 71. It will allow you to see visually one example of how to format your resume product and what we are talking about, thus making it easier for you to understand and apply my advice. Don't miss the important notes about the resume and cover letter examples on pages 72 and 73.

Having an objective is a really good idea. For one thing, anyone hiring has a need and the first question in their mind is: Does your want fill my need?

If you want to be a teacher and the employer is looking for a used car salesperson, you may not have much to talk about; but if the opportunity has anything to do with teaching or teaching skills, then the potential employer is moved to read on.

Another reason why an objective is important is that you do not want to be a wandering generality; it's far better to be a meaningful specific when it comes to getting hired.

To be a meaningful specific, you should have the education, training or specific experience to back up your interest in the position.

Get Two Things Done With Your Objective

You want to do two things with your objective: project direction and posture.

Direction is important because virtually all successful people give direction to their lives, which is probably one reason why they succeed more quickly than people who lack direction.

If you really want to lessen your chances of getting hired today, go into a place and say, "I don't know what I want to do or what I am qualified for, but I am a fast learner, and if you give me an opportunity at anything, I'll pick it up quickly."

Companies and organizations are now less willing to train people for positions than they were in the past, and especially during recession times. Now they want to hire people and have them producing on the job immediately.

Gone are the days when college graduates would get on with a corporation and then spend several months or a year to get their feet wet before they were really expected to know what they were doing, and generate profitable production toward the corporate effort. In too many cases it has now become produce without training or be gone.

30

There simply are too many prospects waiting in line that may bring more experience, education and training to the job equation, and produce faster.

They may also project more **posture and confidence,** two qualities that can help get you hired ahead of your contemporaries.

Posture is important because people think about us what we think about ourselves. If you are a confident person, you are likely to project your confidence through body language as well as what you say and how you say it.

Posture is important too because, if you notice, there is no lack of followers. The vacuum is always in leadership. People are only too anxious to follow a leader, hence employers are looking for leadership qualities even in non-leadership roles.

Leaders are not only self-motivated; they can motivate others. Leaders have initiative. Leaders are committed to getting the job done. They make everyone around them better. Let your posture reflect leadership and you will get ahead farther and faster.

Keep Your Objective Short and Focused

I recommend you condense your objective to a few words and put it in bold face with capital letters.

Examples might be: Administrative Assistant, Customer Service Representative, Production Manufacturing, Receptionist/Bookkeeper or Sales and Marketing.

Skip a line and then put a short, upbeat paragraph using one of two approaches.

The first approach--for business or private enterprise--is:

"Available to accept a challenging Administrative Assistant position where strong organizational, communicative and people skills generate positive results, promote quality service, and enhance company profitability and success."

The second approach--for public service organizations--is:

"Available to accept a challenging Administrative Assistant position where strong organizational, communicative and people skills generate positive results, promote quality service, encourage community support, and enhance organizational success."

If it's a business, you want to enhance company profitability and success; if it's a public service organization, you want to enhance organizational effectiveness and generate community support.

Here is an example of a really poor objective:

"A position which will use my skills and abilities and allow for advancement based on my performance."

It's simply too vague and self-centered. Don't be afraid to put yourself in a career field or industry. Remember, you do not want to be a wandering generality, you want to be a meaningful specific.

There is also no percentage in being self-centered rather than other-centered. You should take the eye off of yourself and put it on the business you are trying to get on with. They do not care about your interest in being advanced because of your amazing talents; they want to know what you are interested in, what you have to offer, and what you can do for them.

The basic objective I am suggesting can be easily modified to better fit what you are trying to accomplish. Here are some examples of changes you could make:

If you know the position doesn't require strong analytical skills, then say "where strong technical, organizational and communicative skills" or "where strong administrative, organizational and communicative skills". If you know the position requires strong customer service skills, then say "promote customer service" rather than "promote quality service".

Both of these approaches not only imply that you can fill the requirements of the position (where strong analytical, planning and communicative skills), but also imply you can help the business (promote quality service and enhance company profitability and success), or organization (promote quality service, enhance organizational effectiveness and generate community support).

I call this Ed's Rule of 3. When crafting your objective, give them no more than three functions you are interested in (Sales, Marketing or Sales Management position), three traits you are going to bring to the table (strong organizational, communicative and people skills), and three things you are going to accomplish for them (produce positive results, promote quality service and enhance company profitability and success).

Part 9

Why the Summary of Qualifications Is Important

Next comes the Summary of Qualifications. The summary is important for three reasons:

First, by using a summary you will get to your potential employer (the reader) quickly with key traits and skills you have to offer.

Second, by using a summary you will need less job description when you get to the Professional Highlights element; remember, we are doing a single page resume product here, space is at a premium.

Third, the summary gives you an excellent opportunity to demonstrate your business sense by relating to what the potential employer is looking for in an employee.

Some young college graduates figure a degree alone is going to net them a good paying job and a secure future. They do not realize that, beyond education, people skills are not just a nice option to have; **people skills are mandatory** if you are going to relate to people and get ahead in the marketplace.

What You Should Cover in the Summary

You do not have a lot of space to list key points in your Summary of Qualifications, so get at least three things done.

When you have experience and accomplishments, use them first and always.

First, use a line that indicates the nature and time of your experience, for example:

"More than 20 years of successful experience in sales and marketing with 10 years in sales management."

Second, let them know your accomplishments, for example:

"Increased sales territory revenue 300% in 18 months, from $500,000 to $2 million."
"Earned Rookie of Year Award, and Annual Top Sales Producer Award twice in 3 years."

Third, let them know you have the people skills to work with anyone, for example:

"Can deal effectively with people of diverse cultural and educational backgrounds."
An awareness of diversity and language skills are absolutely impressive in today's marketplace.

But what if you are just starting out and do not have accomplishments to trumpet? Then do this:

First, use a line that includes vital traits needed for the position, for example:

"Excellent administrative, organizational and communicative skills."

If you're a skilled laborer, modify it to say:

"Excellent analytical, technical and mechanical skills."

Second, cover people skills in your next line. For example:

"Able to interface with administrators, professional staff and clientele."

If you're a skilled laborer, modify it to say:

"Able to relate effectively with supervisors, technicians and skilled craftsmen (or skilled laborers)."

Third, use the next line to cover your initial qualifications:

"Earned a 2-year Certificate as an Electrician from Bates Technical College."

If you have been working for 20 years, but only have 6 years in your career field, you might write:

"More than 20 years of successful experience in dealing with people of diverse cultural and educational backgrounds."

Or, if you have 20 years of experience and 6 years of supervisory experience, try this:

"More than 20 years of successful experience in dealing with people of diverse cultural and educational backgrounds, with 6 years of supervisory experience."

Don't be afraid to capitalize important words in your resume to give them attention. I typically capitalize any job title that refers to my client and frequently capitalize key words in various sections of the resume to give them emphasis. **There is no right and wrong in this regard; it is simply a matter of style, just be consistent.**

I recommend that you do not list character traits--such as honest, dependable and trustworthy--in your Summary of Qualifications.

These are certainly excellent traits to have, but mentioning functions, rather than character traits, is going to get you an interview faster. Functions include administration, organization and communication.

If administrative, financial, supervisory or management skills are not what you have to offer, then use skilled craft/manufacturing functions. Examples would be analytical, technical, electrical or mechanical.

If space allows, and it is appropriate, you could add a couple more lines. Examples might be:

"Able to take charge of situations and deliver results," or "Work well under pressure and against critical deadlines."

The rule on resume writing is really simple: If you **have** awards and accomplishments, you do not need to give fancy or lengthy job descriptions. If you **do not have** awards and accomplishments to talk about, you had better write very good job descriptions.

Job descriptions are pretty useless in most cases because you are not going to educate the person interviewing you on what you have been doing on your job. In most cases, they know what you have been doing. What they really want to know is **what have you accomplished?**

In short, awards and accomplishments trump everything else. There is no competition. **Success counts, job descriptions do not count for squat.** Job descriptions are what you give when you have nothing else more important to give.

Part 10

How to Handle Your Educational Background

Your fourth consideration is your Educational Background.

In the United States, it is a really good idea to have a college degree. A master's degree is better than a bachelor's degree, and a bachelor's degree is better than an associate's degree.

If you have an associate degree, don't get hung up on it; you are a college graduate. People can fuss about the fact that you have a two-year degree rather than a four-year degree, but what they can't fuss about is the fact that you have a college degree.

If you do not have a degree, you definitely want to be in the process of getting one. In this country, it never pays to be anti-education.

Therefore, list all of your degrees beyond high school (such as an associate or bachelor's degree) and your high school degree if you have anything at all going for you.

When listing every degree you have (if space is available), don't be shy about including your accomplishments in school. It should be a given that you would start with your highest degree first.

If you have a degree, handle it like this:

"Bachelor of Arts Degree in Business Administration".

There are places in your resume where you want to use bold face lettering to draw more attention, and listing your degrees is one of them.

On the next line, list the college or university you attended and the city and state where it is located. For example:

"University of Washington in Seattle, WA".

If your degree has a concentration, list it like this:

"Concentration in **Management Information Systems**".

Then list important accomplishments (awards, scholarships), activities and athletic involvement starting with a bullet or some similar bold device on each line.

Include your extracurricular activities (clubs and organizations), if you were a class officer (junior class president, associated student body officer or student council representative), or extracurricular officer (Spanish club president or drama club officer), or played an instrument in the marching band, concert band or orchestra.

Use these items to indicate involvement and achievement at both the high school, college and graduate level.

Examples you could use if they apply:

"Served as President of the Senior Class".

"Served as Vice President of the Drama Club and Secretary of the Local 4-H Club".

"Played Clarinet in the Marching Band and Concert Band".

If you had any involvement in athletics, list the varsity sports you competed in (varsity football and varsity basketball, for example), any leadership roles (captain of the team), any individual recognition (all-league or all-state team selection), and if the team you competed with won any titles (league, district, regional or state titles). **Examples** you could use:

"Competed in Varsity Football, Basketball and Track".

"Served as Captain of the Varsity Football Team During Senior Year".

"Selected as an All League and All District Shortstop in Varsity Baseball as a Junior and Senior".

"Helped Lead Varsity Football Team to the State AAA Title During Junior Year", or

"Competed as Tight End on State AAA Runner-Up Varsity Football Team".

If you financed your own college education (that is, if your parents didn't foot the bill), and worked full or part-time while earning credits, I believe it's important to share the information. Handle it this way:

"Financed Own Education - Worked Part-Time While Earning Degree". (Notice the item doesn't start with a bullet or star; use the bullets or bold face stars for school-generated activities and achievements.)

Then give your cumulative GPA (grade point average) for each degree if it is 3.0 or better on a scale of 4.0 and, of course, when you received your degree.

If you get really pressed for space, try this technique for placement of your GPA and when you received your degree:

"Bachelor of Arts in History - GPA: 3.0".

"University of Washington in Seattle, WA - Degree Awarded in 1994".

Or reverse them if it fits better:

"Bachelor of Arts in History - Degree Awarded in 1994".

"University of Washington in Seattle, WA - GPA: 3.0".

Learn How to Say a Lot Quickly

Try to keep the items to a single line if possible; it promotes readership and you are less likely to get carried away with your verbiage.

Never underestimate the power of accomplishments by individuals or teams.
There are thousands of very important people in very important positions in our country who have achieved academic, leadership, extracurricular or athletic success at the high school or college level and can identify with winners in a heartbeat.

Some clients fuss at me about even mentioning their high school experience, but I think it is a mistake not to if you have something to mention.

A client might say, "Well, what does this crap have to do with the price of tea in China? Really, it's not important."

I may say to them: "Look, here you are, the president of your junior class. That's your classmates saying they want you to be their leader. That's an indicator of leadership ability with a following." Don't underestimate these kind of success indicators early on.

When writing resumes, the idea is to put you head and shoulders above your peer group. Having accomplishments and achievements is an excellent way to separate you out from the crowd.

What to Do If You Do Not Have a Degree

A major concern for many, many clients is that they may have attended college, but they never really earned a degree of any kind.

Some clients may have more than three years of credits toward a bachelor's degree, but never finished and never bothered to see about using the credits to get an associate degree so they would at least be a college graduate.

When you have more than enough credits to earn an associate degree, but not enough for a bachelor's degree, **always** investigate what you would need to do to secure an associate degree.

A two-year college degree makes you **far more marketable** than having three-and-a-half years of credits with no degree at all.

Always try to be street smart about marketing yourself. Remember a degree, **any degree of any kind, is always better than no degree.**

If you attended college but did not graduate, by all means let the employer know.

Some clients feel that if they did not graduate from college, they should not mention it because it shows a failure to complete a commitment. This is nonsense.

I strongly disagree with this kind of thinking. Showing you at least started on a degree means you are trying to improve your knowledge and skills, and that's important. Another factor is the fact that many people work full-time and go to school part-time. People drop out of college for many legitimate reasons: they may need to support themselves, they may be financing their own education and simply run out of money, they may get married, have babies or need to move for family or personal reasons.

38

If you do not have a degree, but are still taking credits toward a degree, list it this way:

"Working on an **Associate of Arts Degree in Business Administration**", or "Working on a **Bachelor of Arts Degree in Business Administration**".

If you do not have a degree, and have been out of school for years, list it this way:

"Work on an **Associate of Arts Degree in Business Administration**", or "Work on a **Bachelor of Arts Degree in Business Administration**".

You do not need to list when you attended college. When you graduate, you absolutely need to list the year you graduated.

List everything else (activities, athletics, accomplishments, achievements) I discussed earlier just as if you had acquired a degree.

For example, maybe you have two years toward a bachelor's degree and your GPA is 3.4. That's important information to share because it shows that, while you may not yet have your degree, you are a quick study (you can learn things quickly).

It's Not What You Say, But How You Say It That Counts

Always remember that **more important than what you say** in a resume **is how you say what you say.** This may sound like double talk, but I tell clients now I'm talking experience, expertise, language skill, knowing what to put in, what to leave out, and why.

If you do not have a degree and are really hung up on this qualification, remember this: **A person of experience will never be at the mercy of a person with book learning.**

All of the degrees in the world might not help a person when he or she gets to the job site.

I have done many resumes for $60,000 a year managers who lack a college degree, but have dozens of employees with bachelor and master's degrees working for them.

They were the boss--not because they had a degree--but because they knew how and what to do when it counted. **Experience matters more than having a degree.** A degree says you have the potential to do something, experience says you have already done it.

One such manager without a college degree, when asked why he was the boss and had many college graduates taking orders from him, said simply:

"Mostly, it's just common sense. When I leave the office at night, I make sure the lights are out and the doors locked. Sometimes folks with degrees are absorbed in their own knowledge and not really paying attention to what's going on around them, and how they fit into the total picture."

Again, a degree says you have the potential to do it (complete a task at the job site); experience says you have already done it.

Get Involved So You Can Achieve Success

The single most important thing for students to do while in school, and especially high school, is to achieve some degree of success at some activity.

Students who never have a feeling of success are in for a tough time in life. A feeling of success in academics, extracurricular activities or athletics builds self-confidence, self-esteem and self-worth.

Success in school breeds success later in life and is an excellent indicator of how people will do when they hit the workplace.

If I have a client who's winning in life today, it's easy for me to go back in his or her background and find a person who was winning 5 years ago, 10 years ago, in college and in high school. It sounds harsh, but **winners win and losers don't.**

You have heard the expression: Never kick a man when he's down.

A good friend of mine says, "When a man is down, kick him as hard as you can; if he lays there and whines, he's a loser; if he gets up a fights, he's a winner."

Some people don't know they are winners because no one has ever given them a chance or challenged them to do something greater with their lives. **You can bet and win almost every time on this:** Winners respond and losers are filled up with excuses.

Remember also that no matter how smart you think you are, that everything looks easy until **YOU** have to do it. Then you find out what they did not teach you at that fancy college you attended. Do not misunderstand me here. I have a bachelor's degree and some graduate study. I believe everyone can benefit by having a college degree. But I also recognize that there is a huge difference between book learning, and doing a task in real time on the job site.

There simply is no substitute for experience. When you see someone with a degree really struggling on the job, you will better understand what I am saying.

Will You Be Exonerated in a Court of Law?

Consider this situation: You are in a court of law as the defendant. You are on trial for being a loser. I am your defense attorney. When I write your resume product, my job is to collect enough evidence to convict you of being successful so you will be exonerated.

I do this by presenting enough factual evidence to paint a picture of a winner about to move on to his or her next challenge in life.

What do you do if you are not a college graduate?

How to Make Money Without a College Degree

It is worth pointing out that many times there is no significant correlation between education and income. One can statistically show that a college graduate, over the course of his or her adult working life, will make more money than a high school graduate who does not go on to higher education.

The problem is that many times the difference between the two is not that great of a difference. It's not like all college graduates make an average of $100,000 a year and all high school graduates make only an average of $30,000 a year. It is more likely that the college graduate is making $60,000 a year, and the high school graduate $40,000.

I understand that if you are a doctor or an attorney, well placed and competent, you are going to make a potentially huge income compared to people who do not have a medical or juris doctor degree (a degree leading to a high-paying profession).

But what about all of the college graduates without professional degrees who end up at McDonald's while they are trying to find a challenging, good paying position that interests them? **Clearly,** without a college degree that leads to a high paying profession, you cannot expect to knock down the big bucks.

Some clients come to me with a bachelor's degree, have been out of school for 10 years and are making less than $35,000 a year. You are going to have a hard time convincing them that a college education has put them on easy street. The reason they are making only $35,000 a year is not because they are underpaid; it is more likely because they are underemployed.

Know How to Market Yourself

Clients in this position generally do not have an education problem, a training problem, an intelligence problem, or a refusal to work problem. They usually have a marketing problem. **They simply don't know how to market themselves.**

Just as there is many times no significant correlation between education and income, so is there no significant correlation between intelligence and income.

There are educated idiots everywhere. A high I.Q. does not automatically equate to a high income.

Many times there is also no significant correlation between talent and income.

Have you ever heard of the proverbial starving artist? How many talented actors have gone to Hollywood and, like thousands of others, not been discovered?

How can we then explain why I have clients who earn more than $100,000 in annual income and do so with a high school degree, and sometimes even without a high school degree?

The answer is that you can show a significant correlation between people skills and income.

In almost every case, if you show me a person who is not in a high paying profession, doesn't have a college degree and makes $100,000 plus a year, I will show you a person with obvious people skills.

Choose People Skills Over Grammar

If a college graduate were to engage an uneducated but high-earning client of mine in conversation, he or she might notice that my client lacks subject-verb agreement when speaking.

Or perhaps my client's diction or enunciation is not correct; however, my client will likely relate to people because he has learned a more important skill: how to understand others and make himself understood.

My client will likely be more other-centered than self-centered, better able to gauge a person's mental and emotional state, and therefore act and speak more appropriately.

People skills are more important than your education, training, experience, talent or intelligence.

The higher you go up the income scale, and the higher you go up the job responsibility scale, the greater the need for people skills.

People who rise to the top do so by using people skills to complement whatever else they bring to the job hiring equation (that is, education, training, experience, talent and intelligence).

Part 11

Specialized or Professional Training Means a Lot

Specialized or professional training, our next element, should never be overlooked in writing a resume.

If you have any specialized training beyond your formal education, include the training you have received or knowledge you have acquired.

If the training happens to relate to the opportunity you are interested in, great; if it doesn't directly relate, include it anyway. Do this because it shows you are an open spirit (willing to learn), and capable of being trained.

Include as specialized training anything you have done on your own nickel, such as attending a Dale Carnegie Human Relations Course, or anything any employer or organization has done to give you additional training.

The latter could be something as simple as cashier training when working for a grocer or retailer or seminars or workshops you have attended on any subject matter.

Include any military training, whether it relates to the specific opportunity or not, especially if it is a school or course you have completed and received a certificate of training. Obviously, if space is an issue in a single page resume, you would not list military training if something else is more important. Many prospects have received expensive specialized training in the military that would cost civilian employers thousands of dollars if they were to give them the same training; thus, you can save your employer big bucks in some cases.

What Specialized Training and Licenses Show

If you have taken and passed a test and received a license to sell real estate or insurance products (life, health, property or casualty insurance), but no longer work in the industry, or never did work in the industry, list the training and licensure anyway.

Do this because it shows you have smarts. There is no way someone is going to receive a real estate license with half a brain in his or her head. It's simply not that easy to pass the test. Very, very few people (you could count them on one hand) could pass the test without reading and studying the material necessary.

Always remember that the less formal education you have (that is the fancy way of saying the fewer degrees you have), the more important the specialized training is, and the more technical it is, the better.

Let's say you don't have a Bachelor of Science Degree in Computer Science and you are a Computer Programmer, Systems Analyst or an Information Systems Manager.

The fact that you may have taken specialized training in a less popular computer programming language or studied how to set up LAN (local area network) systems may be critical to the hiring process.

Most companies want employees who can help them today without training. The company would ideally like to have you productive and contributing to its goals and objectives from day one instead of training you.

Part 12

How to Handle Your Professional Highlights

Call your work experience or employment background "Professional Highlights"; it just sounds so much better, and it implies there is something professional about you (if not your vocation, then at least your work habits).

If you have little actual work experience, you should still be adding value to what you have done.

One way to do this is to call what you have done Professional Highlights.

List your employer first or, if you have been in business for yourself, list your business name. I do this in italics to set it off; but again, there is no right or wrong way, it is simply a matter of taste.

List the location of the employer next. I use city and state only; I see no point in listing specific street addresses with zip codes, and certainly not the phone of the business or organization, which someone could call.

Listing specific addresses only invites the employer to drop a verification or recommendation form in the mail, which, unfortunately, for too many clients would not be such a hot idea. It is just a bad idea to list specific addresses and phone numbers, period. **Don't do it unless you enjoy inviting trouble.**

Don't do it for the same reason you would not send references with your resume, and that is: If they can read your resume, check your references and, on that basis, make a decision not to interview you or hire you, you have done yourself a great disservice.

You want to get in front of people where you can use the force of your personality and verbal skills to sell yourself.

Use the next line to **list your job title in bold face type**, using caps (capitals) and lower case letters.

Using bold type will help the title stand out, which is an even better idea if the title has any substance (Manager, Assistant Manager or Section Supervisor, for example).

Clients Can Get Confused About What Is Important and What Is Not

Some clients want to make where they worked more important than what they were doing. Make your job title more important than for whom you were doing it; better to be an Assistant Manager at a local restaurant than a Clerk for a K-Mart unit.

When describing what you were doing (your job responsibilities), it's best to start with the phrase "Responsible for . . . ".

The effect of this is to constantly remind the reader you are a responsible person, doing something responsible in a responsible position.

And, while what you do specifically is important, even more important is what I call **"facts and figures".**

By this I mean anything that as a direct result of your effort has increased a company's or organization's revenue, increased its net profitability, or reduced its overheads.

As mentioned earlier, accomplishments, achievements and awards are far more important than job descriptions. If you have them, you could start with this:

"Recognized for . . . " and then immediately start listing your accomplishments, achievements and awards.

This (facts and figures) is what will separate you out from the crowd, so to speak.

Anytime you can demonstrate to a business that you can **make them money or save them money,** you have two excellent trump cards to come calling on them, other than to say: "I'm looking for a good opportunity. Can you help me out?"

I'll grant you that showing facts and figures is sometimes easier to do in a business climate. If we know, for example, that a company has 12 sales representatives and one sales rep generates 35% of all the sales, we don't really need to ask who's the star of the staff.

If you are in a public service organization (any federal, state, city or county job, school teacher, police officer, fire protection specialist or military person), talk about how you delivered more service for the same budgeted dollars, or were able to increase the case load you were handling, or how you assisted in the conversion of an inventory control system from hand receipts to an automated (computer) system.

Don't be fooled into thinking that public service organizations don't fuss about money too.

In the business world, we talk about P+L (profit and loss) statements; in public service, we talk about budgets. There isn't a nickel's worth of difference between the two.

If public service organizations don't get funded, people get laid off, services cut and departments reorganized.

You Must Be Street Smart About Money

As I examine business, whether it's IBM or Exxon or the local grocery store, and strip away all the tinsel around the underlying motive, I'm left with this thing called greed.

It doesn't sound nice, I grant you, but if you can identify the underlying motive and appeal to it, the chances are you are going to get where you want to go quicker. That's why you must be street smart about how the money system works.

Businesses and organizations need to understand that you know what drives their existence; it is not giving service, it is taking in money to support what they are doing.

Don't let businesses or public service organizations fool you into thinking that they exist to help or serve people; helping or serving people is merely a by-product of generating enough revenue to be in a position to do so.

I don't need to tell you that the world turns on a dollar bill. I'm not judging that, but I am saying we need to be street smart about how the money system works.

How to Get the Employer's Attention Fast

Imagine an employer's reaction if you are in sales and mention that you started in a territory from scratch and built it to $2 million in sales in two years.

Imagine that same employer in the same industry doing $2 million in annual sales, and he or she is wondering how to increase sales.

Now don't go making things up that are not true. Absolutely use every money issue that is positive, but also have the track record and substance to back it up.

I tell clients that I'm good at prose. By prose I mean the duties and responsibilities description, which I am good at, will do, and will sound good.

But, as a professional writer, the resume will be much more effective if it is filled with facts and figures; I mean positive money comments and how it will affect the potential employer.

In short, money talks. Never forget it; it's what makes the world go around.

Why Career Progression Is Important

Where possible, show career progression visually rather than lumping together all of the titles you may have had at one organization.

There is a proven charm or likeability in starting out as a clerk and 20 years later running the company or organization. Career progression chronicles this happening.

We frankly dislike people who come in on top. Nobody really likes the boss bringing in and promoting his or her relatives above people who have served the organization well and are passed over.

People love success stories, especially where--by the honest sweat of one's brow--they start out sweeping the floors and work their way up to an important position. We like people who pay their dues.

When It Doesn't Work for You

This is the Protestant ethic: work hard, keep your nose clean and good things will happen. Too often today, good things don't happen, which might explain why a lot of folks have little use for the Protestant ethic, or any other religious ethic.

How many times have you seen a fellow employee who was hired or promoted but who wasn't really the most qualified person to be hired or promoted?

Yes, you should be seething too. Someone might say: "I can't believe they hired that person", or "I can't believe they promoted that jerk. If they only knew."

The fact is that **more than 50% of the time, the person hired or promoted is not the most qualified.**

It's really simple. People who hire get a lot of pressure to go through all their relatives, friends, neighbors and lovers to find prospects to hire or promote.

Granted that much of this occurs at entry level to mid-management positions, but it occurs **none the less.**

I do have some good news for you: the people who get hired or promoted are oftentimes not the most qualified, but usually they have done the best job of presenting what it is they have to offer.

This means that many, many clients who are not the most qualified can also get hired or promoted if I do the best job of presenting what it is they have to offer.

Make No Mistake: Whom You Know Does Count

There is no question that **60% of all hiring and promoting has to do with whom you know.**

If I have a female client, I tell her that it's wonderful that she may be qualified for a position, but **the better situation** is if she marries the owner's son. I guarantee you that she will have more opportunity to get ahead.

That's why networking is so important. You always want to be developing what I call mini-friendships with people who can help you down the road.

Since it's a two-way street, make sure you help others when the opportunity arises.

The Importance of Recognition

Once you get by education, specialized training and work experience, and learn the importance of money issues, the next important item on your resume agenda should be recognition.

I don't list it as one of the eight basic elements, but it is very important.

If you have recognition for your job performance, share it by creating a separate category on the left side called "Professional Awards".

Examples might include being named "Sales Representative of the Month or Year", "Rookie of the Year in Sales", receiving a "Sustained Superior Performance Award" if you are in public service, or receiving an award for "Outstanding Customer Service".

Again, anything that puts you head and shoulders above your peer group is what I want to share in the resume.

You can also handle less formal job recognition while tackling your "Professional Highlights" section.

I ask clients to tell me four or five of their best professional or personal strengths or traits. Then, in the copy block, rather than have the client brag on himself, I say:

48

"Recognized for productivity, organization, attention to detail and people skills". Substitute whatever works and makes sense based on what you bring to the hiring equation.

If I can see a client is sharp and with it, many times I will add another sentence that can have tremendous force and effect:

"Position (referring to the client's position) requires (or required if they are in between jobs) technical knowledge, organizational ability and strong communication skills in relating to people of diverse cultural and educational backgrounds".

Companies and organizations need to be paying extensive attention today to equal employment and cultural diversity in their personnel mix.

The sentence suggested above implies that someone is aware of these issues, and has had positive experiences with a diverse work force in the marketplace.

Part 13

What Your Military Background Tells

If you have never been in the military, no big deal. But, if you have, always include some key facts, even if you were in for 2 years 30 years ago.

Remember that many potential employers who might hire you could be 50 or older. If they are, and they are male, they probably can relate very well to you if you have served your country (by choice or by the then draft) and they have served their country.

Two pieces of information are very important in this area.

One is whether you were honorably discharged (nothing else need be said here) and **two,** whether you were awarded a good conduct medal.

Being honorably discharged gives you a big stamp of approval.

Receiving a good conduct medal means you did not dramatically screw up when you were serving your country.

If you mess up--examples are alcohol/drug abuse, authority problems or insubordination--you will not get a good conduct medal and, in fact, you may be asked to leave the service.

Put the branch of service you were in and the fact that you were honorably discharged in bold face, caps and lower case letters. For example:

"United States Air Force - Honorable Discharge".

Tell the years you served. (Again, see the sample one page resume included as a link to this email report.)

Tell what your specialty was; it doesn't matter if it has to do with the opportunity you are pursuing or not.

If you were awarded any medal such as a Commendation Medal, Achievement Medal, Humanitarian Medal, Liberation Medal or higher, mention it because it underscores the fact you are a proven performer.

If you have a Meritorious Service Medal, Silver Star, Bronze Star or Purple Heart, absolutely mention it. There is nothing wrong with heroism. We have too few real heroes today.

It is also important to note if you had a security clearance. Anyone who held a Top Secret or Secret Security Clearance should mention it, as well as any designators for access to go with it, such as NATO (North Atlantic Treaty Organization), CRYPTO (sending and receiving classified messages) or SCI (Sensitive Compartmented Information) Access.

A lot of large corporations have government contracts to do work that require their personnel to have a security clearance in order to do the work.

If you have had a security clearance in the past, the probability of getting one in the future is better and faster.

Some retiring and separating military personnel have security clearances that are good after they leave the military; this can save corporations big bucks and make you a more attractive prospect.

Another important item to mention is if you served in a war or conflict on behalf of your country. If you served during the Vietnam Conflict and actually were in the Southeast Asia Theater of Operation, you are a Vietnam Veteran.

If you served during the Vietnam Conflict, but were assigned anywhere else in the world, you would be what we technically call a Vietnam Era Veteran (this means you served during the Vietnam Conflict, but weren't actually serving in Vietnam or the expanded Theater of Operation). For civilian purposes, you are a Vietnam Veteran; it is not necessary to describe yourself as a Vietnam Era Veteran.

50

It is true that the Vietnam Conflict (it never was a declared war if you remember) was not a popular war and caused a lot of political upheaval.

However, still mention your service to your country. You didn't choose the war or the time you were serving in many cases; you did your part to help your country and should be recognized as such.

The Persian Gulf War was as popular as the Vietnam Conflict was unpopular. If you were serving in the voluntary forces for our country, you would also be either a Persian Gulf War Veteran or a Persian Gulf War Era Veteran.

For any other important purpose, whether you were in a theater of operation or not, your government considers you a military veteran if you served during a time of conflict or war.

You will know if you are in either of these categories if you received a National Defense Service Medal, or other medals or ribbons that indicate your service during these conflicts or wars.

Part 14

Why Personal Data Is a Nice Touch

The last element for your consideration is Personal Data.

Some clients believe that including any personal data in a resume is nonsense; I believe just the opposite: that personal data can offer some pertinent information and help give you needed "balance" when someone is assessing you as a potential hire.

First, I recommend you consider saying: U. S. Citizen. Or, if you are not a U. S. Citizen, say: Permanent Resident; Japanese Citizen (or whatever your citizenship is).

Your citizenship can be important because abuse in hiring (by using illegal immigrants) has forced employers to verify and prove U. S. citizenship before hiring otherwise eligible candidates.

Many large corporations also have contracts with the federal government requiring security clearances which you may not be granted--even though you may be an otherwise qualified worker--if you are not a United States Citizen.

Your Ability to Relate Is Very Important

Second, I recommend you consider revealing your marital status, saying that you are "Single" or "Married".

Single could mean divorced, separated, widowed, live-in roommate or significant other. All your employer needs to know is that you are single.

Married is married is married, which means, until laws specifically change, married to someone of the opposite sex.

If, during an interview process, they want more specifics about your personal relationships, you would have to decide how much more you might want to reveal about your personal life. It is important that you understand that the potential employer **cannot**, by law, ask your marital status. This question is considered discriminatory.

However, I believe it can make sense for you to reveal this fact.

First, by mentioning you are single or married, it doesn't raise any seeds of doubt about your marital status.

Second, if you are married, it can show stability, and that you have even more reason to produce on the job.

Third, if you are single, it can signal that you are perhaps better able to travel or relocate since you do not have a spouse to consider.

Fourth, revealing your marital status up front may save you some grief later on by letting people know you are or are not available--under normal circumstances--for more personal relationships.

Was She Married or Not? I'll Never Tell!

One very successful female executive client of mine insisted that we specify she was "married" in the personal data section of the product I produced for her. She was not, however, married, and clearly understood that this was a question an interviewer could not legally ask.

She was an attractive woman who was simply sick and tired of being chased around the corporate desk (office romance happens everywhere). This was her way of calling off some of the dogs before they got out of the pen. She has since come back for updates to her product, and I flat ask her: "How can you continue to get away with this deception?"

52

She showed me her diamond wedding ring (bought as a treat to herself), and a current picture of her "husband" from her wallet (a really good-looking guy who was really her brother).

I asked: "How do you handle the corporate get-togethers (annual parties and meetings) when people ask why you never bring your husband?"

Her answer: "We have a long distance marriage. I'm here on the West Coast; my husband is a successful sales rep on the East Coast. We have residences in both places. We spend most of our weekends together in the Midwest in another residence of ours. We really have a weekend marriage, and we like it that way."

And you ask why she is a very successful, street smart, resourceful, female corporate executive?

Female Executives and The Liberated Woman

Fifth, female executives and professionals can make a statement about how liberated they are or are not by sharing marital information. Consider this example:

A liberated women is asked her martial status during an interview and responds by saying:

"I'm really surprised that you would ask me that question. In fact, I am really disappointed in your lack of awareness and professionalism. It's really none of your business, and I am personally offended that you would ask me. If this is any indication of the caliber of how your organization conducts its business, I'm not sure I want to even continue this interview."

That, certainly, is one way to respond. But I would have to ask you **how street smart** the response would be.

I would suggest that the answer given is not the best response to what one may find to be a personally stressful question. **Would this person likely be hired? I frankly doubt it.** By revealing your marital status up front you can accomplish two things:

One, you can give the company or organization a piece of information that they cannot legally ask you, which may break down some important barriers.

Two, you can show that you are not so liberated that you would make this sort of question a lighting rod for a call to action if a personnel type was stupid enough to ask. Really liberated women might consider it their duty to lobby the employees to become a union organization during her first week on the job. A potential, non-union employer needs this like they need another hole in their head.

Revealing your marital status may make you a more likeable candidate and make you seem less of a challenge to deal with than if you are super liberated, proud of it and taking no prisoners along the way.

The last person an employer wants to hire is a personality problem, or someone who cannot easily fit into the "corporate culture".

Until you are an employee who is successful enough to own the company and make the rules, you still need to relate to people before you attempt to change the world. **You will change nothing if you do not first relate to people.**

Next, we suggest you share your willingness to travel or relocate. Simply say: Willing to travel or relocate. It is not good to qualify your willingness to travel or relocate by saying: "Willing to travel in-state only", or "Willing to relocate on the East Coast".

You should always be willing to travel since it could mean something as simple as living in one city and commuting to another to work, or it could be as complicated as traveling out-of-state for two weeks every month. There is a very big difference between the two.

Give Yourself an Opportunity to Say No

Recognize that you can always say no to an opportunity. I would rather have you be offered the opportunity and say no than not receive the offer at all.

The idea is to open doors, not close them. After all, you're looking for employment; you're not the employer, so don't put limitations on the process. Let it work for you.

If you are not willing to relocate, then don't mention it. Just say: Willing to travel.

But, before you say no, you are not willing to relocate, ask yourself this question:

If a company offered you a position earning $80,000 a year in another state, would you move? (To answer this question properly, double what you are now making.)

If you answer yes to the question, then you are in fact willing to relocate.

Remember, you can always say no to an offer. If the company fusses at you when you say no, reply this way: "I'm willing to relocate for $80,000 to Portland, but I hear you offering me $40,000 a year to relocate to Tuba City, Montana" (a fictitious town).

The next item should be "High School Graduate" if you did not cover this in your Educational Background section which you would use if you were a college graduate or had credits toward a college degree.

54

If you did not graduate from high school, don't mention it; it simply raises too many seeds of doubt about your suitability for employment.

It may imply that you quit high school (that is, you will not adjust to a challenge and follow through successfully, whatever the problems).

It may imply that you are lazy (simply too lazy to get up off your butt and do something to help yourself and others; in other words, try to succeed).

It may imply that you are illiterate (unable to read and write effectively, and consequently unable to follow written company instructions, or perhaps not effectively relate to customers in your dealings).

Whatever it may imply to anyone, I guarantee you it is nothing good or positive when it comes to your getting hired.

Any Seed of Doubt Will Do You In

This is one of my cardinal rules in resume writing: You cannot do anything that will raise a seed of doubt in the person reading the resume or interviewing you for a position.

And, really now, who among us, if put under intense scrutiny, does not have a chink in his or her armor?

If you didn't graduate from high school and later earned a GED (general equivalency diploma), it is the equivalent of a high school degree, and I see no reason not to simply say you are a "High School Graduate".

If they want to see a copy of your high school degree, show them your GED document.

Next, space allowing, I list hobbies and interests.

This Is, After All, A Relating Process

I do this, not because it has anything necessarily to do with the opportunity you are seeking, but because the person reading your resume and interviewing you has hobbies and interests too.

Remember, this whole business of reading resumes is a relating process, and the better someone relates to you, the greater the odds are that something good and positive is going to happen.

Say you want a job as a teacher and have an interest in aerobics and the person interviewing you is heavy into aerobics, do you think you might talk about it at the interview?

If they are relating to you, it may come up in the conversation; and even if the subject does not come up, it does not mean they did not read the fact of your interest in aerobics and relate to it because they enjoy the activity as well.

Another thing hobbies and interests can show is well being. It is all but trite to say in a resume that you are in excellent health (as if you would tell them if you just had back surgery and will need constant medical care in the near term) when, in the same amount of breath, you could say you enjoy aerobics, jogging, snow and water skiing, bicycling or swimming.

Which method conveys more information and creates more interest?

Last, we suggest this line in bold face, caps and lower case: **Excellent personal and professional references available on request.**

Don't say "References on request" or "References available" when you can use the qualifier "Excellent personal and professional references . . . "

Remember, it is not what you say nearly as much as it is how you say what you say.

That's not double talk. I'm now talking about experience, expertise, language skill, knowing what to put in, what to leave out, and why.

Part 15

Why References Are Overrated

Many clients do not understand that references are overrated in most cases.

It is not uncommon for a potential employer to interview and all but hire a prospect before even thinking about checking references, and when he or she does, it is generally to verify employment only.

Think about it from an employer's perspective. If every resume received had three references listed and they received 400 resumes, does anyone really think they are going to call 1,200 references **before** they determine whom they are going to interview? Let's get serious. They are going to interview first and, and if they like the prospect and want to hire her (or him), even checking references afterward has a diminished effect.

First, they trust their own judgment better than the reference they would call.

Second, they know the prospect is hardly going to give them a reference that is bad. For all they know, it could be the prospect's uncle or best friend.

Take It All With a Grain of Salt

Even when an employer calls and does not get this sparkling review of you, most successful people are smart enough to know that you take everything with a grain of salt.

There are, for example, personality conflicts, conflicts of belief and direction, disagreements about priorities, and how we treat the customers who deal with us. We do not live in a perfect world.

On the other hand, when you do get a sparkling review--they say you can walk on water--we know this may be true, but only when the water is frozen, which in Western Washington on the West Coast is not often.

To review: don't give specific references with your resume.

If they can read your resume and check your references and, on that basis, make a decision to not interview you or hire you, I think you have done yourself a tremendous disservice.

You want to get in front of people at all costs. Giving references up front may only slow you down. You want to plant enough nuggets in your resume to create interest, enough interest so that they have to call you in to interview you to answer all of their questions about your success.

It is for this reason that I believe that references are not appropriate at the resume stage; **references are much more appropriate at the interview stage.**

An interviewer may look at your resume, see the line in it saying "Excellent personal and professional references available on request", and say, "It looks like you have references, can I see them?"

That's an invitation to pull them out, but what do most potential hires do? They pull out a list of names, addresses and phone numbers.

If, at the interview stage, they ask for references--which is appropriate--I highly recommend that you do not give them names, addresses and phone numbers to call. That could be a big mistake.

Consider this example: A client of mine making $60,000 a year in a sales position was going for an $80,000 a year position, and gave the name of Bob Brown as a reference to call.

When the company called the reference, a voice came back saying, "Bob Brown? We fired him last month."

There is no way my client could have known. When he had left the company a year ago, Bob Brown was the star sales rep on the staff.

In the meantime, a new general manager was hired, had a personality conflict with Bob Brown and, rather than being smart about it, let his ego get out of control, and conspired to undermine Bob Brown for about 5 months before he could drum him out of the company. This can, and does, happen more often than you might think. The point is you think you know what someone is going to say about you if an interviewer calls; the fact is you do not have a clue.

Why It Is Smart to Always Give Written References

What else could possibly go wrong with giving names, addresses and phone numbers?

For one thing, it inconveniences the potential employer. They then have to call. If, when they call, the person on the other end of the line has had a bad day, they may be snotty, or put them on hold, or cut them off completely.

A voice could come back saying, "We don't have a Bob Brown working here" (the personnel type may be too lazy to get up and look in the files if they do not recognize the name; perhaps the person in question moved on from the business a year ago).

Another voice could come back saying, "Mr. Brown is on vacation. Would you like to have him call you when he returns in three weeks?"

Your answer to yourself is: No, I'm hiring this week. I'll check another equally qualified candidate's references. I think you can see the problems clients seldom think about.

The message is: If you give references, *always* give written references rather than names, addresses and phone numbers. Here are the housekeeping details: **One,** have the person giving the reference put it in writing. **Two,** have them do it on official looking stationary (the letterhead) of either the business or organization. If it is against their company policy to do it on company letterhead, then suggest they do it on a blank sheet of paper. They can still sign their title and company at the bottom. **Three,** have them sign it. Never give away the original, always make copies to hand out.

A Written Reference Is Good Forever

People come and go; they get married and divorced; they have babies and leave the work force; they get promoted or transferred and leave; they develop health problems and leave. All sorts of things happen to people. Written references are good forever.

They are good forever because frozen in that moment of time is the person's personal or professional opinion about you. Use it for the next 30 years if you can; don't worry about the date on the written reference.

And here's the kicker: When you give someone a written reference, 99 times out of 100 they accept it at face value: they expect it to say something good about you and it does.

This puts you more in control of the situation, which is what you want to be (at least you know what someone is saying about you if it is written).

Three or four written references should be enough. If you can't get professional references (about your job performance), then get personal references (about your honesty, integrity or community service activities).

When they call after receiving a written reference, it's usually to verify employment.

There is nothing to preclude someone from calling even though you give them a written reference. Usually the name, address and phone number of the business will appear in the letterhead at the top of the stationery.

Normally, however, there is a requirement to get two references into the personnel file before they make an offer. If you give them two written references, what do you think they are going to do? Probably put them in the file and not bother calling, especially if they interview you, like your personality, and believe you can do the job.

When References Must Be Impeccable

There is one case where they will check references and that's when the position involves money, as in large amounts of American green (not negotiable instruments, like checks, stocks or bonds) passing through your hands every day, and you are responsible for counting it, and it does not belong to you.

If you apply for a position like this, have impeccable references.

But also remember that members of the Mafia who are educated and in "legitimate" businesses, can write outstanding reference letters too.

Now you understand why references are overrated.

When checking references for fiduciary (money) positions, go ahead and check them, **but always** call the state patrol or other law enforcement agencies to see if the applicant has a police record for fraud or embezzlement.

Part 16

How to Handle Cover Letters

When you read job announcements or opportunities online or in the newspaper, almost all of these ads say "send email resume to" and do not ask for a cover letter.

If they do not specifically ask for a cover letter, do not email your cover letter. You will just irritate them.

Occasionally, they may specifically ask for an "email resume and cover letter". Other announcements may ask for a "letter of interest" or "letter of qualification".

No matter what they might call the letter, they are all really the same.

If you want to prove this point, call the company and ask them to explain in detail the difference between a "cover letter" and a "letter of interest" (if that's what they are ask for).

I've actually done it, and you never heard someone on the other end of the phone back pedal so quickly, hem and haw and generally look silly and unprepared. They really couldn't tell you the difference if their life depended upon it.

When you are able to mail a hard copy resume, always include a cover letter on top of your resume.

I can't sit here and tell you the resume will not work by itself; I just know it's going to work a lot better when you include a cover letter.

Of the two, **your resume is far more important than your cover letter because** it gives the reader more and better information about you.

Unfortunately, when announcements ask only for the resume, most clients feel compelled to write a cover letter to explain why they are sending the resume.

Usually, in the process of doing so, they hurt themselves more than help themselves.

The reason why is, while not meaning to do so, they too often come across sounding self-centered rather than other-centered.

They get hung up by saying I, I, I rather than you, you, you.

The idea is to get the eye off of yourself and onto to other person, or in this case, the business or organization presenting the opportunity.

Why Cover Letters by Clients Don't Usually Work

A case in point is a typical cover letter written by a client. It goes like this:

"I read your ad in the Sunday *News Tribune* and would like to apply for the position of Administrative Assistant.

"As you can tell from my resume, I am well qualified, have tons of experience and I have always been loyal, dependable and hard working.

"I am really interested in your company and I feel that I can make an immediate contribution to your success. I have the administrative skills you are seeking. I would like to interview for this position. Please feel free to call me 24-hours-a-day, 7-days-a-week collect.

"I will look forward to hearing from you so I can set up a time for an interview. Thank you.

"Sincerely, Jane Doe."

To repeat the message: The word "I" was used 10 times in this relatively short cover letter.

The trick to writing cover letters is you have to get out of the "first person" (the use of I) and instead write in the "third person" (not using I, as it is one of the strongest words in the English language).

This is difficult for most clients to do because they have been raised from birth to respond with "I" when someone says, "What do you think?" It's just really natural and normal to respond with "I think . . ."

In the case of cover letters, you would be well advised not to.

I know if I gave my clients a homework lesson to write a cover letter and use the word "I" only once, that **not 1 in 100** could probably do it in an artful way. And, since I am in the high end of the business, these would be clients who are mainly well educated, have important positions, and earn big incomes.

Ninety percent of my 5,400+ active clients are executives or professionals, who normally earn between $50,000 and $140,000 annually, and are in management or supervision.

They do poorly on cover letters simply because they don't have a lot of practice at writing cover letters; it's not that they can't write, or are not educated. Not to mention the fact that, whether they recognize it or not, they are emotionally involved and always tend to underestimate or overestimate what they have to offer.

Therefore, I recommend that clients do not write cover letters. Cover letters can be very valuable to clients, but if they need them, I recommend that they have me do them. If we are going to go through the cover letter drill, we can get more done if I do it.

If you need a cover letter, hire a pro to do it for you.

Another huge mistake is the killer last sentence, which says "I will look forward to hearing from you so I can set up a time for an interview. Thank you."

The sentence is presumptive in that it boldly marches forth to an interview without an invitation. That's bad form.

Even worse is to say "I will call you next week to set up an appointment for an interview". The latter is not only presumptive, but intrusive. It demonstrates almost a total lack of people skills.

Also, what is this business of thanking people when, at that point, they have done nothing for you?

The Purpose of a Cover Letter

I believe the purpose of a cover letter is to do one thing and one thing only: and that is to **demonstrate people skills.**

Most clients believe the purpose of the cover letter is to tell the employer why they are sending the resume, or rehash what is in the resume, or what specifically they have to offer.

A far better use of the cover letter is to demonstrate people skills, and that means severely limiting the use of the word "I" as it can send the wrong message.

You need to show the employer how you can help grow their business or organization.

Tell them **not what** you have to offer (25 years of sales experience) **but how** what you have to offer can benefit them (increased annual territory sales 40% within 8 months).

When you are showing the employer how you can help grow their business, do it with people skills.

Remember, I talked about the only correlation involving income worth talking about was the correlation between people skills and income.

Play on that theme (people skills) and you will put yourself head and shoulders above the crowd.

Part 17

What to Do When They Ask for Salary History

Some announcements ask for a resume and salary history. You need to know that when this happens, it is a good bet the advertiser is trying to buy cheap.

If a corporation has a position budgeted for $40,000 and they can find someone who appears qualified, is raring to go, and has never made more than $30,000 a year, they have no problem with offering them $35,000 for the position and, of course, all the experience they can get!

They play on your lack of experience, confidence and posture.

When you bite for the $35,000, they can move the extra $5,000 they would have spent to other needs, or simply add it to net profit for the year. This is why the personnel manager can sometimes look as good as the sales manager.

If you ask them why they want a salary history, they are going to get excited (you are not supposed to question their request, and they just might take umbrage if you do).

They would likely give you an answer that was not an answer, or simply say their salaries are competitive with the industry.

You need only check about two places in the industry to find out they are not competitive, and that's the biggest reason for the game playing.

Send the Resume, Skip the Salary History

Send your salary history if you want (what you have made in the past, and perhaps future salary requirements), but understand what is going on here.

I certainly don't recommend you **ever** send your salary history with a resume.

Send your resume **without** your salary history. When you do this, one of two things will likely happen.

One, they receive your resume with no salary history and say, "Look at this dummy, we asked for a salary history and he never sent it. If he or she can't follow directions, why should we hire him?" At this point, they may throw your resume in File 13 (the wastebasket).

Two, they will read your resume anyway. When they do, it's amazing how they can figure out your phone number and call you if they like what they read. The odds say that 9 times out of 10 they are going to read your resume even if you don't comply with their request for a salary history.

This makes sense if you think it through.

For one thing, they are looking for and need "good" people. Of course they would like to hire them as cheaply as possible, but they will pay what they have to in hiring the people they really want.

Ed's Cardinal Rule No. 1

Another important point to remember is that **people who read resumes are not nearly as dense as clients generally think they are.**

I know clients think people who read resumes are dense because, if asked a question by an interviewer, they tend to answer the question, and then they feel compelled to explain or justify the answer they have given.

This especially happens if one has only a high school education and feels the lack of a college degree is really hurting her or him in the hiring process.

Give resume readers some credit. They are basically bright people who can figure things out too.

When writing resumes, I always invoke **Rule No. 1: Assume the person reading the resume is at least as smart as you think you are.** And you know how smart we all think we are.

Never underestimate the intelligence of the resume reader, and never overestimate his or her knowledge.

In other words, give them an abundance of facts and let them figure it out.

To summarize: Giving your salary history with your resume is like playing poker and showing everyone your hand before the bidding starts. It is **never** a smart idea, and it can only hurt you.

64

Learn and Practice Ed's Zip-a-Lip Theory

I want to digress a moment and return to my earlier statement about how clients answer interview questions (that is, they answer the question and then feel compelled to explain or justify the answer they are giving).

This is an absolute no no.

The single biggest mistake clients make during an interview is to answer a question and then rattle on.

I have interviewed and hired many people in another place at another time, and I can tell you from experience that many clients talk themselves into a job, and then 10 minutes later they talk themselves out of a job by what comes out of their mouth.

They simply don't know how to answer a question and then **zip-a-lip.**

If the interviewer wants more information, force him or her to ask a more specific question. Then answer the question, and again, zip-a-lip.

Treat job interviews like IRS audits (Internal Revenue Service). Answer the question and then shut up. You have heard the old saying that it is better to remain silent than open your mouth and remove all doubt. It is certainly true during interviews.

I've asked prospective employees a job-related question, and 2 minutes later they end up talking about their sled dog trip to Alaska. Word association causes clients to get side-tracked, and it can absolutely kill their chances of survival in an interview.

Associating Appropriately Pays Huge Dividends

The more times in an interview when you can smile, and yet remain silent when it is appropriate to do so, the more intelligent and in command the interviewer is going to think you are. It is mostly when you open your mouth at inappropriate times that you open Pandora's box and get into trouble.

Part 18

What Employers Are Looking for in a Prospect

Most potential employees are told that employers are looking for someone with a degree and hands-on skills.

While this is true in many cases, you should know that employers are also looking for someone who can do the job. This is why they are not necessarily looking for someone with **only** education, experience and knowledge, as important as these three attributes may be.

Some employers will not hold it against you if you do not have education, experience, knowledge or obvious ability going for you. For some prospects, the ego is so well developed that an employer cannot teach them anything because they already know everything. (If you have a teenager in your household, you likely know what I mean.)

The ego, in this case, becomes a barrier to learning.

It is really helpful to be an open, willing spirit without all the answers; and this applies whether you have education, experience, knowledge and ability, or you do not. While employers **may not** hold it against you if you do not have education, experience and knowledge, **they will hold it very much against you** if you have a poor personality and cannot get along (work) with people.

People Skills Are Not an Option

In other words, **the single biggest thing you have going for yourself is people skills.** It is more important in the long run than education, experience, knowledge, talent and intelligence.

Some clients feel people skills are an option; they are not an option: **people skills are mandatory if you expect to get ahead in this world.**

When you greet customers or fellow employees, the last thing a business or organization can afford is for you to cost them customers or the support of other employees because you are a negative person who cannot get along or work with other people.

Believe it or not, **the two most important qualities** you have going for you are 1) Your personality (which is based on your attitude), and 2) Your ability to deal with people effectively.

If you show me someone with a bad attitude, I will show you someone with a bad personality. If you show me someone with a good attitude, I will show you someone with a good personality. In short, personality does not drive attitude, attitude drives personality. If someone has an obnoxious personality, I will show you someone with a poor attitude.

Therefore, it makes all kinds of sense to sell yourself in an interview **before** you sell your education, experience, knowledge or special abilities.

It will do the employer no good to hire God's gift to the job if he or she cannot get along with customers and their fellow employees.

If you do no more than learn how to smile, act enthusiastic and act interested in people, it may well take you farther than the knowledge of an expensive college education with a bad attitude.

Persistence Does Pay Off

As you move forward in your quest to reposition yourself (get hired) in the marketplace, always keep your eye on your objective: securing interviews rather than securing a job.

Remember that an interview almost always precedes the actual hiring. Keep your thought process and mental attitude on securing interviews.

In the meantime, I recommend the following words of wisdom to you from none other than former President Calvin Coolidge: he certainly knew something about securing a position:

Press On

"Nothing in the world can take the place of persistence. Talent will not; nothing is more common than unsuccessful men with talent. Genius will not; unrewarded genius is almost a proverb. Education will not; the world is full of educated derelicts. Persistence and determination alone are omnipotent."

Check out my websites:

1) **Quality Resumes by Ed Bagley**
at: http://quality-resumes-by-ed-bagley.com

Offers Quality Resume Writing and Job Counseling Services with Ed Bagley and His Time, Talent, Experience and Expertise in Helping Market Potential Hires. Ed Works With You Personally. An Author and Professional Writer, Ed Has 25+ Years of Experience and Has Helped 5,400+ Clients Acquire New Jobs.

2) **Ed Bagley's Blog**
at: http://www.ed-bagley-blog.com

Ed Bagley's Blog with his news, coverage and commentary as a writer, author, newspaper publisher and book publisher during the past 50 years.

3) **Ed Bagley's Blog Archives**
at: http://ed-bagley-blog-archives.com

Ed Bagley's Blog Archives has his first 971 original articles on 54 different subjects covering 69,000+ pages, including coverage on college football, college basketball, track, distance running, movies, business, marketing, family, relationships, life, faith and politics. Did I forget to mention humor?

4) **Ed Bagley's College Football**
at: http://ed-bagley-college-football.com

Ed Bagley's College Football has a 14-Week Wrap-Up of Major 2011 College Action, Complete 2011 Bowl Game Coverage, and the 2011 National Championship Game Synopsis. Next up is the Pre-Season Coverage for the coming year. Go to Ed Bagley's Blog Archives for complete NCAA coverage on the 2007, 2008, 2009 and 2010 seasons.

5) **Ed Bagley's Northwest Marketing Program**
at: http://ed-bagley-northwest-marketing-program.com

Ed Bagley's Northwest Marketing Program is the home site for Northwest Marketing LLC, an umbrella company in the State of Washington under which several business activities happen, including 7 commercial web sites, a brick-and-mortar upscale writing service, a book publishing company, and a marketing company.

ED BAGLEY

Expert Writer and Marketer
Quality-Resumes-by-Ed-Bagley.com

P. O. Box 3658
Lacey, WA 98509

Telephone: (800) 000-0000

Extensive experience as a writer, editor, author, publisher, marketer and business manager, online expertise, and relevant education has led me to formulate the following objective:

Writing, Editing and Marketing opportunities where effective organizational, analytical and communicative skills generate outstanding writing projects, produce positive results, provide quality customer service, and advance a client's professional and personal growth.

My overall background includes 30+ years of successful experience in dealing effectively with people of diverse cultural and educational backgrounds, currently as an Expert Writer and Marketer for the new start-up Quality-Resumes-by-Ed-Bagley.com, providing an upscale resume writing service, and developing products to help unemployed and underemployed potential hires find opportunities. Prior experience includes:

- Being a managing editor, sports editor and investigative reporter for daily newspapers, an editor or managing editor for 7 weekly newspapers, a newspaper publishing company owner, a niche book publishing company owner, marketing company owner, creator of an online articles website, and creator of a jobs and careers online website.

- Becoming one of the youngest managing editors of a daily newspaper in the United States at 27, one of the youngest publishing company owners at 31, and being the youngest panel member for the first ever joint meeting of the National Newspaper Association and the Canadian Newspaper Association in Toronto, Ontario, Canada.

- Winning 7 national awards, 2 international awards and 5 state awards for excellence in journalism, and helping set a national record by converting a 1,500-paid letterpress weekly into a 10,000-paid offset daily as Managing Editor of the Westfield (MA) Evening News.

- Serving as a Newspaper Editor in Colorado, Libya, North Africa and Germany while on active duty in the United States Air Force during the Vietnam Conflict.

- Earning a Bachelor of Arts Degree in Journalism from Michigan State University, and competing on Michigan State's NCAA cross-country and track teams.

Taking on new challenges, being open to change and having a strong desire to help others succeed are, for me, prerequisites for continued success. I am open to opportunities. Call me.

Sincerely,

Ed Bagley

ED BAGLEY

_____professional profile

P. O. Box 3658
Lacey, WA 98509
Telephone: (253) 000-0000

Objective:

WRITING, EDITING or MARKETING OPPORTUNITIES

Available to accept Writing, Editing or Marketing opportunities where effective organizational, analytical and communicative skills generate outstanding writing projects, produce positive results, provide quality customer service, and advance a client's professional and growth.

Summary of
Qualifications:

▸ More than 30 years of successful experience as a writer, editor, author, publisher, marketer and business manager.
▸ Spent 20 years in the newspaper business, and 24 years operating a writing service.
▸ Won 7 national awards, 2 international awards and 5 state awards for excellence in journalism, and helped 5,400+ upscale clients get hired during 24 years a professional writer and marketer.

Educational
Background:

Bachelor of Arts Degree in Journalism
Michigan State University in East Lansing, MI - Awarded in 1966
▸ Middle Distance Runner for MSU on Cross-Country and Track Teams.
▸ Editor of 2 Weekly Newspapers While Attending School Full-Time.

Professional
Highlights:

Quality-Resumes-by-Ed-Bagley.com   Tacoma, WA
Chief Writer and Marketer   2011 to Present

Recognized for helping 5,400+ clients get hired then joined this start-up.

Northwest Marketing LLC   Lacey, WA
Expert Writer and Marketer   1981 to Present

Successfully operate a writing and marketing service concentrating on upscale clients interested in high-end positions and upward mobility.

The Lacey Leader   Lacey, WA
Editor and Publisher   1973 to 1981

Recognized for editing a weekly newspaper and managing the daily operations of a community publishing company.

Prior Experience includes serving as a **Managing Editor**, **Sports Editor** and an **Investigative Reporter** for daily newspapers, and an **Editor** or **Managing Editor** for 7 weekly newspapers.

Military Background:

United States Air Force - Honorable Discharge   1967 to 1971
▸ Served as an Award-Winning Newspaper Editor and Info Specialist.
▸ Held a Secret Security Clearance - Qualify as a Vietnam Veteran.

Excellent personal & professional references available on request.

71

Important Notes About the Single Page Resume and Cover Letter Examples:

Because of the layout constraints of this book, the Single Page Resume and Cover Letter examples on pages 70 and 71 do not appear as they normally would. They were modified to fit so they could be included in this book as examples. Here are some suggestions to make writing your Single Page Resume and Cover Letter easier:

1) Set your margins for the both the Resume and Cover Letter at one-half inch on all four sides. The margins in both examples are set at one inch on all four sides. If you are in an older version of Word (such as Word 97, for example), set your header and footer for 0".

2) You should make sure there are no hyphenations in your copy. Hyphenating words is not cool, and should be avoided.

3) The lines on your copy should be ragged right rather than justified.

4) There is no need to set indents for your Resume. Your tab is probably set for one-half inch, so put in "Objective:" and simply hit your tab key 3 times and you have the equivalent of a 2-inch indent from the left margin.

5) Use 12 pt. Arial Bold for your name, and 9 pt. Arial for the rest of the copy.

6) Under "Professional Highlights" after you put in the name of the company, push the city, state info over until it is flush right. This will help frame the page as it will agree with the address and phone number near the top of the page, which is also flush right.

7) It is important to remember that there is no right or wrong way to write a resume. The style you choose and the words you choose to represent are simply, and importantly, a matter of judgment. Be consistent with your usage. Some words can be capitalized or bold-faced for emphasis, even though if you were following the rules exactly, you would not normally do so. Again, there is no right or wrong. You are making an impression, so try your best to be neat and tidy about what you are doing.

8) Remember that the quickest way to increase readability is white space, so don't be afraid to use white space to make your resume more readable.

9) The second paragraph of the Cover Letter example is indented on every line on purpose. The second paragraph is a repeat of your objective on the resume, and it is presented differently to draw more attention to it.

10) Try, as much as possible, to stay out of the passive voice (past tense) when using verbs. The strongest verb form is present tense "ing" (not managed but managing, not delegated but delegating), and using this puts you in the active voice.

11) You want to repeat important points from the resume in the cover letter. Do this because, if the resume and cover letter were to get separated in the hiring process, someone important reading the cover letter only would know that they want to interview you without seeing your resume.

12) Notice in the cover letter that the word "I" appears exactly one time in the example. Clients who write cover letters for themselves use the letter "I" numerous times in the cover letter, which is not a good idea because it comes across sounding self-centered rather than other-centered. Clients do not mean to do this. It happens because when we are asked a question, we are taught to respond by saying "I (this or that) . . . " Clients end up in the first person because they do not know how to get out it, and put themselves in the active voice (present tense). Notice how I do this in the example, and you will be able to avoid using "I" in your cover letter.

This ends the book. If you have learned something by reading it, and it has been of value to you, do not be shy about going to Amazon.com and writing a positive review of the book for me. Remember that you cannot do a kindness too soon, for you never know how soon it will be too late. After all, I am 68 years old and I am not going to live forever (if you are not smiling or laughing, you should be). I wish you the best. Stay alert. Stay happy. Be healthy. And enjoy life, it's free.